He Had Me At Meow

The Story of an Irresistible Rascal
and the Gal Who Loved Him

Chari Fish

Ten|16
PRESS

www.ten16press.com - Waukesha, WI

To all the cats who have wrapped themselves around my heart through the years...and to Cooper's Angels.

TABLE OF CONTENTS

Chapter 1 **SEDUCTION**

We women know when we've locked eyes with an irresistible *bad boy*. That's when we're most vulnerable and inclined to act impulsively.

On a golden October afternoon in 2010 I snaked through a maze of kitty cages at the Humane Society of Marathon County. I'm not sure what drew my attention to the one above my head, other than the singular obsession to locate the perfect companion for my cat, Chloe.

And there he lay, an adorable ball of peach-colored fluff, dozing away the afternoon. Maybe his dream had just ended because while I stared, a green eye inched open. When he discovered a stranger ogling him, the other eye followed. As if he read *Sucker* on my forehead, he arched his back and stretched his stubby arms toward me so I'd notice the stylish white mittens adorning his front paws and the distinctive white line that kissed the crest of his pink nose.

I'm sure he identified me as the perfect accomplice for his jail break because he rose completely and turned in a circle, allowing a panoramic view of his snowy underside and the six white rings that decorated his foxy tail. To seal the deal his left paw stroked the glass where I'd placed my hand, and his faint meow beckoned me closer.

"What's your story, fella?" I whispered, reaching for the bio attached to his enclosure. He head-butted the glass. It worked; full attention restored. The gleam in his eye said *I can reel this one in.*

"I see you still have your 'boys.' If you want to come home with me, it's snip-snip, little buddy." When he didn't burst into flames, I knew my voice hadn't penetrated the glass. I scanned the room for someone who could release him into my arms.

"Excuse me," I said to the young brunette who had just finished a phone conversation. "May I take that little guy into one of your empty rooms?" I pointed at him. Having gained the full attention of two women, he overlooked my rude gesture.

"Reddy?" she asked.

They named him Reddy. How unimaginative. But we can work on that. "He bewitched me," I admitted.

"He's a cutie," she said, a smile brightening her face. Don't know why he hasn't been adopted yet; he's been here a while."

"Does he have a rap sheet?" I asked, only half-kidding. "He thumped his head on the glass when I tried to read his card."

She chuckled. "A lady who'd been feeding him brought him in as a stray. She said she would have kept him but already had two cats, and they didn't drop the welcome mat. He's really friendly and good with both cats and dogs, so he must have had a home. We figure he's about one to two years old."

The instant she placed him into my arms, he settled against my chest and revved his engine; the sturdy rumble felt like a high-powered vibrator.

He's so cute, so perfect. He's gotta have a defect.

As if he'd heard my thoughts, Reddy shifted his position and dewy green and gold eyes begged for a home. I melted inside his gaze, already a goner. No need for play time, although I sensed he'd welcome an opportunity to run a few laps or shred a toy to protest his incarceration.

When I put him down in what must have looked like kitty play land, he took off like a tornado. The little whirligig spun around the room and slid from corner to corner on the slick linoleum floor, pouncing on everything stable enough to withstand his exuberance.

It was time to re-direct his energy. I slid to the floor beside him and batted at a ball on a track in a plastic circle. Reddy belly-slid to the other side and whacked the ball back to me. We enjoyed this give and take for a while, then I snatched a feather toy attached to a wand that looked like a fishing rod. He sprang into action, leaping to great heights to attack the offending feathers. I noticed a woman peering at us through the glass door, mesmerized by our interaction. Danger flashed; this little scamp, who had so thoroughly captivated me, was now amusing my competition.

Go away, my eyes implored.

There was no time to waste. Reddy was still in play mode, but I swept him up and carried him to the front desk, breezing past the woman I saw as an interloper and kissing the heck out of Reddy's cheeks. I wasn't about to relinquish him to another. He was good about being carried, and his little motor was still on high while he took in the sights. I'm sure he had an inkling something good would come of this. We were already color-coordinated, his hair and mine almost a perfect match.

Anyone who has ever visited an animal shelter knows that most of the time it's noisy, chaotic, and malodorous. This day was no different, and I couldn't find anyone to help me begin the adoption process. It would have been so nice to just back out of the place with my prize - especially since he'd tossed me a conspiring grin that said, *Let's boogie.*

A tall gray-haired woman approached us. "Do you want me to take Reddy?"

"No, we're good," I said, "but I'd like to fill out an adoption application."

"You're the sixth applicant interested in him," she said.

"What?" I saw my newest love slipping away. "If five others are ahead of me, I'll never get him."

"Order doesn't matter. We try to place each animal in the best home."

Reddy helped me fill out the form, applying his paw prints to each page. I hoped having his DNA on my application would give me an edge. One of the questions was *Where will your pet sleep?* That was silly…in bed with me, of course. Maybe having adopted Chloe there in August would work in my favor.

It was finally time to surrender my precious bundle. We were now in wait mode, and I was anxious to get home and chat him up to Chloe.

***

Ah, Chloe. Her story wasn't so rosy either. She began life as Chai and had a companion named Mocha. A family had relinquished the two cats, along with two dogs because they were moving. My favorite cat breed is the Main Coon and my initial visit was to find one. When I spotted Chloe, her size, Sasquatch paws, and markings indicated Main Coon lineage. Lying next to her was a small brown, peach, and cream-colored tabby. The thought of breaking up two cats who were bonded never entered my mind.

Into an empty room they went with me. Both girls were friendly and sweet, but I called in an attendant when Mocha retched and vomited pink drool. I filled out adoption papers and all went well until the day I was to pick up my new kitties. The Humane Society called to tell me they had euthanized Mocha because she'd tested positive for feline leukemia and was showing signs of liver failure. Although Chloe tested negative for the dreaded disease, she would need to be re-tested in a couple of weeks. They asked if I still wanted her. Of course; she needed me all the more having just lost her companion. Although I was devastated at not being able to give little Mocha a good home, I wanted Chloe more than ever.

The evolution of Chloe's name came about by chance. Chai seemed harsh for such a sweet girl; Chloe fit her. She warmed to the name and wore it well within hours. We were a happy pair, and she was the teddy bear who slept in my arms every night. I wanted her to have another companion, a kitty to snuggle and play with when I wasn't around.

Chapter 2   HELL HATH NO FURY

After a grueling wait, one in which I felt certain I'd lost my little guy to another family, the call came that he was to be mine. Off to PetsMart I dashed to purchase a red leather carrier, replete with sheepskin interior for this new addition. And, of course, he would need a few toys to enjoy with Chloe and me. The feather toy on the wand was first, quickly followed by a few catnip mice and a Chase Track, that plastic toy with the balls on a track. We'd had such fun with that one. I'd already made a catnip sock for Chloe that I was pretty sure she'd frown on sharing. I'd have to make Reddy his own. Together, the little man and I would choose the right name for him.

I'll admit to feeling a bit of trepidation at the first meeting of my two new cats. In retrospect, tossing them together was a rather uninspired idea. Reddy was game; he ran right up to Chloe and touched her nose. She acknowledged his friendly greeting by hissing in his face. She followed this rudeness with a whack to the nose, then she dive-bombed him and pummeled his head. The little guy couldn't get away fast enough. He sped through the house like the devil was after him. And, in a way, she was. I hoofed it behind them shouting for peace. This was a side of Chloe I couldn't believe existed.

The attacks continued for exactly one week. Poor Reddy leapt into my lap for protection each time Chloe's eyes glazed over. I often saw a perplexed expression on his little face that said *She could use psychiatric help.* I was a bit taken aback when he seemed to suggest cementing her into the wall. I took the smile on his face as a wry sense of humor and let it slide.

Finally, thank the good Lord, Chloe seemed to acquiesce to the fact that her new brother was a permanent fixture, and she'd need to make a few adjustments. After two weeks, she was in love. As for Reddy? He could take her or leave her.

Being the only male in the household, he quickly established himself as the crown prince. This title came with certain privileges. The first was dining from Chloe's food and water bowls because they were more convenient than walking the extra couple of yards to the other side of the china cabinet where his own resided. Chloe's most precious toy suddenly became his, and she was to immediately surrender it whenever he found favor. Her ideal spot atop the kitty condo soon became his. Although he would sometimes share with her, he just as often pushed her off in order to stretch out and gain the best vantage point through the glass slider to the bird feeder. If I were dense enough to place only one paper bag on the floor and Chloe was first inside, the little man had only to stand at the entrance for a moment or two, tilt his head to one side in annoyance, and Chloe would vacate. She often huffed at his ungentlemanly behavior but never retaliated. I was frankly amazed at how quickly the role-reversal had taken place.

Chapter 3   **BECOMING COOPER**

Is there anything more important than a name for your cat, taking into consideration, of course, that all his other needs are being met?

I know I looked psychotic crouched like a troll and dogging Reddy's tracks calling out names to test his reaction, but I live alone; no one here to judge me.

"Prince Charles? Prince William? Prince Harry? How 'bout Samson? Cody?" Then I tried great lovers from literature. "Rhett Butler? Heathcliff? Mr. Darcy?" He only ran faster. It was time for movie idols. "Clark Gable? Robert Redford? Brad Pitt?" I called, rushing along behind him. After a few irritating minutes of this, he turned and shot me his testiest scowl. His face folded into a look of consternation that said *Take it down a few notches*.

"You kinda look like a Cooper," I threw out. When he sat on his haunches, I took it as a sign. Phew…the crown prince had chosen his name.

> Cooper's Rule:
> If you break things at night,
> convince your mom she did it
> while sleepwalking.

Chapter 4 THINGS THAT GO CRASH IN THE NIGHT

To be truthful, life with Cooper sorely tested my endurance. Like a toddler, he ventured into everything. Mayhem welcomed me home if I were out for any length of time. Chloe didn't have to point at her brother for me to learn quickly who was the Mad Hatter in our household.

At first the disturbances were so minor he psyched me into believing I was responsible: open drawers, dish towels askew, and slightly tipsy books. When I arrived home to open cabinets, hot pads and pans on the floor, and plants teetering on the edge of a table, I knew Cooper had been a busy boy.

The dark of night brewed bedlam. Soon after Cooper became a member of the family, he seemed to register that my insomnia had subsided, and I was finally at rest. It was nearly 3:00 a.m. when a shattering c-r-a-s-h wrenched me from dreamland. Still slightly unconscious, my first thought was that a rapist or murderer was inside my house. When I heard the skittering of tiny cat claws racing across hardwood floors in the living room, I knew the intruder was four-legged and furry. Grudgingly, I struggled out of bed to determine what had become the sacrificial lamb in my living room.

The plant inside my favorite porcelain pot was on its side on the floor at the entrance to the dining room. It was surrounded by damp soil and broken pottery. I couldn't leave the mess until morning lest one of my babies sever a paw. I cleaned up the clutter and by that time was wide awake. My night of sweet dreams was short-lived.

Two evenings later, a slightly muffled crash emanated from my home office when Cooper toppled a plant from my desk onto the printer. It was my great pleasure to clean dusty plant soil from the inside of my HP. After this became a popular sport of his, I relocated all plants to the top of the refrigerator.

"I should have named you Dennis the Menace," I told him, pushing the last plant to the wall in back of the fridge. He lifted his strawberry head and studied me as if to say *Do you really think I can't get up there?*

When he seemed to have grown weary of tossing plants, the caterwauling began. Throughout the night he ran from window to window yowling to whatever friend or foe, real or imagined, tormented him. I often joined him at the window but could never see the phantom of his fixation.

To any cat behaviorist who may be reading this, I assure you that I played with this boy every day in an attempt to wear him out so he'd sleep the night away with Chloe and me. Chloe even joined in the effort by playing chase with him daily. At bedtime, he zonked out on his back, hind legs splayed wide and front paws tucked engagingly under his chin…in the middle of my legs. He must have known I can't stand anything touching my legs when I'm in bed. In moments he was snoring like a drunken sailor and looked like the sweetest angel. But, no matter, his biological clock ticked to 3:00 a.m. and alarm bells rang. Up and off he'd trot to do the devil's work. I worried he'd think his name was NO. It was the word he heard most often in relation to himself.

Each time I threatened to take him back to the Humane Society, Cooper jumped into my lap and turned his powerful motor on full-blast. I could expect a few raspy licks from his sandpaper tongue and a soft rub on my forehead. He was the rogue whose charm melted my heart. He also garnered 90 percent of my attention by becoming the squeaky wheel.

After a few weeks with my new adoptees, I took several photos of Cooper and Chloe to the Humane Society, along with a twelve pound bag of cat food to donate. While the ladies ooh'd and ah'd, I told them Cooper was the naughtiest cat I ever adopted, emphasizing that they'd made the right choice for him. No one else would have kept the wily rascal for long.

Cooper's Rule:
If you're a Tarzan enthusiast,
make sure a sturdy vine
hangs nearby.

Chapter 5   **THE GREAT ESCAPE**

Anyone who knows me will tell you I've always been a firm believer in keeping cats inside. I owned a condo in Seattle for twenty-one years and became the willing slave of four cats during that period: Sasha, CoCo, Bailey, and Kady. Keeping them inside was a no-brainer since I lived on the second floor of a security building. They luxuriated in the comfort of a wood-burning fireplace in the living room. Behind it, I hid a large kitty condo. Solarium windows flanked the fireplace on three sides, and the cats enjoyed a semi-panoramic view of the outdoors and plenty of sunshine. They lived long lives and were perfectly content.

Kady, the last of my Seattle cats, flew in the cabin with me when I moved to North Central Wisconsin in 2003 to care for my elderly parents. She was nearly fourteen when we arrived and lived to be slightly over nineteen. After she died, I lasted a mere four days without a cat and adopted Chloe. I had added a deck to my single-family home here in Wausau and thought it might be nice if the kitties joined me out there for a little siesta in the sun whenever the spirit moved them. Chloe was the litmus test and only ventured as far as the deck and the fenced back yard. Like many bird watchers, she had a favorite tree under which she observed her feathered friends as they built their nests and chirped to each other about matters only birds could appreciate.

Cooper's reaction to once again being in the great outdoors was different. When he stepped over the threshold onto the deck, his eyes expanded to embrace the vastness of his heavenly landscape. His head bobbed up and down to the rhythm of the many intriguing scents his nose followed…and he bolted. Flying down the steps, he darted around the house and was gone from sight before I could don a pair of shoes and follow him.

How could I not know the little bugger would fly the coop? I live in town, and Eighth Avenue fronts my house. Wausau is tiny compared to Denver, Los Angeles, and Seattle, my three previous locations. Not one skyscraper pierces the clouds, and downtown is just a stretch of the legs from my house. However, a four-lane thoroughfare sits a block away and across that is Marathon Park and the UW-extension. As a former stray, Cooper would have developed some *street smarts*, but he didn't know the neighborhood. Now my seriously delinquent cat was missing and could be anywhere.

I can only imagine the expressions on my neighbors' faces when they caught me stumbling through the neighborhood shouting, "Cooper!" in an oversized T-shirt (hopefully a bra), flip-flops and pajama bottoms. But who can think about anything as mundane as wardrobe when your child is missing?

For two hours I scoured the area spitting out his name like a lunatic, panic rising with every unsuccessful moment. Another hour was wasted in the car. Finally, I parked in the garage and trudged back onto the deck, tears of frustration wetting my face.

"Coo-per," I called, exhausted and hopeless.

"Meow."

"Cooper?"

"Meow."

It had to be Coop answering me; he knew his name. He was close, but I wasn't sure which neighbor's yard he was in.

"Cooper!"

I listened intently.

"Meow."

I leaned over the deck railing and strained to hear. It sounded like he was in my neighbor, Ted's, driveway. Relief flooded my body, and I sprinted like a racehorse to Ted's property and called one last time, "Cooper." Two peach arms stretched into view from under Ted's trailer hitch, quickly followed by a little face and two sorrowful eyes too embarrassed to meet mine. He fell onto his back and glanced at me upside down, stretching his cuteness to the max. I could hear his mighty pur-r-r.

"You got lost, didn't you, buddy?" He came to me and I picked up my love, gave him a hug and kissed his cheeks hard enough to make them pink. Two tuckered beasts clung to each other and sauntered home.

***

After our little adventure, I determined Cooper would be an inside cat. He determined otherwise. He became the madman no one wants to encounter. He raged against confinement, bouncing off walls and yowling for a breath of freedom. If a door to the outside opened by so much as a crack, he morphed to fit through it, and scooted out to Mother Nature's bounty.

I tried pleading my case to him, hoping to convince him to stay inside. He shot me the same squinty face a baby makes just before he projectile vomits. I interpreted it to mean *You'll have to come up with a more compelling argument.*

"What can be more compelling than life and death?" I asked. He showed me his backside and marched out of the room.

The sound of a can opener drew both cats, but it was Cooper I needed to bribe. As they ate white albacore tuna in water, I tried a new tactic.

"Hey, Coop. How about I let you go outside if you promise to stay in your own yard?"

No reaction. This was his way of letting me know his freedom could have no restrictions. He was going to win and he knew it. It was all too obvious that keeping Cooper inside killed his spirit. If it's true the eyes are the windows to the soul, I saw a candle in each of his that shone as bright as any star when he glimpsed the open doorway to his outside wonderland. But believe me, every time that little guy left my yard, I aged a couple of years. Until he was safely by my side, I never felt completely secure. On the upside, he quickly learned the neighborhood and was never lost again.

Cooper's Rule:
If you enjoy a rooftop view, avoid eagles.

Chapter 6   **KING OF THE WORLD**

The first time I glanced out the slider and saw Cooper on the roof of my garage, I needed adult diapers. Evidently he did, too, because he was franticly darting from one end of the garage to the other in search of a safe route to the ground. The only accessory to his folly that I could see was the French lilac tree to the left of the garage. The little monkey must have climbed the tree and jumped from a limb onto the roof.

In 2010 I was sixty-two years old and disinclined to try my luck on a rickety ladder to save a cat who should never have gotten on the roof in the first place. I figured he'd eventually find a way down. Eventually wasn't happening; he'd been up there for an hour. My effort to coax him back to the tree with tuna had no effect. Coop was in a panic and the way he was tap dancing, I figured he was seconds away from a jump. Frightening scenarios taxed my imagination. It didn't help when I recalled seeing an eagle in a tree across the street a week before. All I could think about was a raptor swooping in and carrying away my precious boy. I retrieved the ladder. Now both of us were in jeopardy. I'm a girly-girl; under normal circumstances, I don't do ladders. Like "Jack," I took tentative steps up the beanstalk. Cooper was on the ledge above the garage door until I reached it. That's when he backed away.

"I'm trying to save you, ya dork." His face scrunched into an expression that said *I have zero confidence in your ability to see us both safely to the ground.* That made two of us. This felt like mountain climbing 101 without a safety harness. We did a dance for a while longer and my expletives turned blue. Then Cooper straddled the ledge like he was about to step on the ladder and make his own way down. I saw my chance and grabbed him by the scruff of his neck. "Gotcha." I bent down and swung the little scamp as close to the ground as I dared and unceremoniously dropped him on the grass. A couple of new gray hairs sprouted when the ladder slipped just before I reached the bottom. I leapt to safety moments before it fell.

"That's the last time I'm risking my life for you, buster!" I shouted once we were back on earth. He hunched his shoulders and slunk away, duly chastised. And it *was* the last time I needed to rescue him. He often climbed the French lilac tree and loved being high up on the roof of the garage where he could scrutinize his kingdom. When he wanted to disembark, he simply vaulted onto a tree limb and clambered down. It wasn't long after that when I saw him spring from the top of my privacy fence to my neighbor,

Ted's garage, even higher than mine. He climbed to the summit and proudly announced, *I'm king of the world!*

> Cooper's Rule:
> Don't fret if your mom can't appreciate your trophy.
> She doesn't understand the ways of the jungle.

Chapter 7   ON SAFARI

Soon Cooper guided Chloe on safari into the dark regions of our back yard, where wild creatures lurk, and only the most skilled hunter can draw them out. Often I spied the two conspirators crouched side-by-side in the grass, focused like a laser on some small prey.

Chloe knows nothing of hunting (bugs don't count). She's the *I'll carry your gear* person. She is also an intense and adoring observer, who fell completely under Cooper's spell. He was her Lancelot, the bright knight who escorted her into the most exquisite adventures. I kept an alert eye on them in the event I needed to hone my rescue skills.

One day, it was a small mouse spinning in the air and cartwheeling through the grass. Another, it was a baby bunny I scrambled to rescue. On a day when I left the slider open so they could wander in and out, I was surprised by a baby Mourning Dove that Cooper brought me as a belated Mother's Day gift. He made the presentation on the rug in front of my kitchen sink with much pomp and circumstance. I praised him mightily, then returned the dove to its tree. Five minutes later, they were back. Cooper's face deflated like a balloon at my lack of good manners in not gobbling up his plump offering. By this time I gleaned the dove was injured and carried it out onto the deck to inspect it more closely. I was relieved when it wriggled from my grasp and flew away. Five minutes later, they were back. This time Cooper's whole body shook with exasperation as if to say *Will you please just eat it, wear it, or hang it on a wall?*

It was time to call in the troops. After sequestering the hunter and his lady, I scurried to my basement and found a box that could comfortably house the dove. I rolled a small clean towel into a log for the bird to perch upon, and phoned my neighbor, Pat. We put our heads together and found the telephone number and address of a lady who worked at the raptor rescue in Antigo. She instructed us to bring her the bird immediately so she could administer antibiotics. We did as she requested, and this story ended happily. I called a week later to check on the dove and was pleased to hear she was with two other baby Mourning Doves and recovering nicely. Cooper was unappeased; he didn't get to see me eat, wear, or mount his gift.

***

The little man in my house never believed me when I told him the reason he must stay inside when inclement weather hit was to keep him safe, dry and warm. Wisconsin can suffer some pretty scary electrical storms. Thunder booms like canons from hell, and winds ravage the landscape and blast sheets of rain in every direction. We were having just such a storm when I walked Cooper to the slider and opened it, so he could feel the pelting of an autumn squall.

"See? It's horrid out there," I said, as if our nerves hadn't already been battered by the storm just sitting inside.

Cooper burst out the door, dodged flashes of lightning, and raced to the garage. The access door was cracked open. He watched the storm from the doorway, then watched me watching him. I stared, incredulous at his bold stupidity.

This is gonna pass, the flicker in his eyes implied, *and I've gotta be ready to roll.*

Mother Nature has a sense of humor when an animal is trying to gain the upper hand. Shortly after our standoff, the storm passed, and the rain trickled out. My rebellious boy strode out of the garage with his tail and butt in the air and his head held high. *Who's the stupid one now?* his stance suggested just before he tore out of sight.

My neighbors quickly became acquainted with Cooper. He was a friendly fellow and inclined to visit for a spell if one of them was working outside. Still, he never let anyone outside the family get close enough to touch him; he was savvy about safety. Since I didn't know how wide his territory was, I knew the importance of his having a breakaway collar. I added visible ID and a warning chime for wildlife after he began his sojourns outside. Our Humane Society microchips all pets when they're adopted, but even Chloe was fitted with a stylish pink glitter collar and heart-shaped tag, and she never left the back yard. If she were outside playing with Cooper and he scooted under the fence, she watched him longingly but never followed. For this small recompense, I was most grateful.

After Cooper lost thirteen collars, I considered purchasing stock in PetsMart. Neighbors near and far began calling, and the conversations went something like this:

"Hello, this is Mrs. so and so. Do you have a pet named Cooper?

I found his collar on a tree limb…or fence…or in my yard, and wondered if he's missing."

One afternoon my neighbor, Pat, called. "Cooper was here visiting for a bit. He's racing home with something in his mouth."

"Please tell me he's running down the sidewalk and not in the middle of the street," I asked.

"He was on the sidewalk, but he should be home by now."

"I better go see what he has." A glance out my bedroom window revealed my cat plopping a chipmunk onto the grass. I hurried outside and found Cooper playing with it. The chipmunk bit me when I attempted a rescue, but he managed to get away safely. Since he didn't break the skin, I wasn't too worried about rabies. Cooper shook his head. *What the bleep?* I read on his frustrated face.

The unspoken agreement between my little adventurer and me was that 7:00 p.m. was his curfew. Nine times out of ten he observed this rule and was waiting at the slider to be let inside. If his little tushy wasn't front and center at the appointed time, I embarrassed him by calling his name from the deck.

The faint tinkle of his bell preceded him when he loped down the alley behind our house, or scurried across the top of my privacy fence to the deck railing. It wasn't until I heard the jingle announcing his presence that my heart began to beat normally again. When he aged me by sauntering in a couple hours late and I scowled at him, he simply shrugged his shoulders and offered the same tired excuse. *Chill, little Mama. I was just out with my homeboys checkin' the pulse of the neighborhood.*

I was not appeased. But as soon as he crossed the threshold, Coop softened my heart by wrapping his bushy peach tail around my leg (his signature hug). Then he trotted to his food bowl where he waited for love and praise before chowing down. This was a ritual we always observed. His mother, so happy to have him safe at home, smothered him in coos and air kisses, while scratching his back. It was the cherished hors d'oeuvre he relished before his evening meal.

Once Cooper was inside for the night, our routine rarely varied. He enjoyed lounging on top of the couch. The little man gazed out the window into the front yard and kept tabs on the action. If things were slow, he watched TV. Coop became *my* entertainment when he flew off the couch to smack at something on the screen that was stirring enough to garner his attention. The commercial where a cat bats at falling leaves against a wall drew him in one hundred percent of the time. If the TV cat couldn't master those leaves, Coop nailed them every time. Just before exhaustion folded his eyelids, he'd crawl into my lap and allow as many kisses as I could pucker; the deal was that I scratched his back at the same time. In moments he was zonked out and snoring. Not long after, I lugged him to bed.

Of course, the best television was the Nature Channel or Reality TV for Cats. This mode of entertainment could best be observed from their perch atop the kitty condo. The conduit was the glass slider, which provided a glimpse into all that nature could provide: birth, death, and the stories in between. It was free and always available. And it could only be surpassed by actually stepping into its magic.

***

As a certified *clean freak* with two cats, every day can be one of drudgery. Chloe is blessed with a plume tail that attracts everything like a magnet. After a morning in the dew-blanketed back yard, she came in and made her way throughout the house, swishing her tail from side-to-side. Pine needles, slugs, worms, and other small creatures that found a ride on her tail attractive, dropped off at different locations throughout my house. I often found myself in the middle of a debris field. If I wasn't close behind her with a vacuum or a broom as Chloe meandered, my eyes constantly scanned the floor for movement.

One afternoon I experienced a moment of cardiac arrest when I entered my home office and confronted what appeared to be a long, skinny snake drying out on the carpet. Upon closer inspection, it turned out to be the largest earthworm I had ever encountered.

"Cooper. Chloe." I heard the thunder of cat feet charging from the living room and, no doubt, hoping for a treat. When both my children stood before me with blank faces, I asked the pointed question. "Who brought in the Jurassic worm?" It was too large to fit on Chloe's tail. Someone had brought it in, and I had a darn good idea who that was. I wondered if he'd give himself up. Four innocent eyes stared into mine. I glared back.

Bored and unintimidated, they broke ranks and wandered to separate pursuits, leaving me to deal with disposal. Using a tissue to avoid any intimate contact, I picked up the worm and tossed it over the deck and onto damp grass. That guy probably fed a family of robins for a week.

> Cooper's Rule:
> Nothing good comes from trapping
> a cat inside a cardboard box.

Chapter 8 NEVER TAKE A CAT THROUGH A CAR WASH

Sometimes the planets just don't align for us, our lives lose harmony for a time, and chaos ensues. Cooper and I endured such an occasion when I saw the need for a visit to our vet. My little man had developed a red, scaly rash between his shoulder blades.

I had loaned both my leather cat carriers to a friend who needed to pick up her new adoptees from the Humane Society. I kept an old cardboard carrier in the basement as a backup and used that to transport Cooper.

The problem wasn't with our visit to Dr. Kuhn's office. Both Cooper and Chloe were model patients; they were completely docile and malleable, probably due to abject terror. My crisis with Cooper evolved from a profoundly idiotic idea to hit the car wash on our way home, a decision on par with sky diving into a volcano.

Slowly cruising into the car wash, not a sound could be heard from the cat inhabiting the box strapped onto the passenger seat of my Honda Prelude. *Piece of cake* I thought as the jet spray hit. Water pelted the car on all sides, much like the roiling spray of river rapids. I heard a rustling sound inside the box. *It's just Coop changing positions*, I told myself. When he began thumping against the walls,

I regretted paying an extra two dollars for the super wash; it would lengthen our stay inside what must have seemed like a house of horrors to my cat. Bulging eyeballs peered out of air holes in the box. I realized that from his vantage point we were underwater, and sea creatures were lashing at the car to get inside and gobble us alive.

A white paw shot out of the hole closest to me, gripped the edge and began tearing; canines joined in, and he gnawed at the hole and tore it open in a frenzy.

"We're okay, Coop. It's only a car wash. We'll be through it soon," I pleaded, feeling like the world's worst mom. All he heard was, "Blah, blah, blah." The little man seemed to believe he could conquer the sea creatures and save us both if he could only free himself. And why was I not helping?

By the time thwacking tentacles began their attack, Cooper's head and shoulders were outside the box, and he was shimmying to freedom. I was stunned and more than a little impressed at the size of the hole he'd managed to gnaw through the carrier in the short time it took us to navigate the car wash. He was on his back on the dashboard pushing all fours against the windshield when the roar of the dryer blew us back outside.

I was sure Coop was just as relieved as I was to see the sun glinting off the windshield. His teeth had rendered the carrier uninhabitable. I just wanted us to get home in one piece. I turned onto Stewart Avenue; that's when Cooper decided to drive. He sprang onto the steering wheel and straddled it. With all fours splayed, he looked something like a hairy starfish.

I was now attempting to drive a car with about ten pounds of cat glued to the steering wheel. While downshifting, I popped the clutch and struggled to maintain my space in one lane of traffic. I prayed for a red light in order to make the necessary corrections.

Just as there's never a cop around when you need one, he's always behind you when you're trying to cover your worst offense. My heart flip-flopped in my chest when I saw one of Wausau's finest looming large in the rear view mirror. The whoop of his siren encouraged us to pull over.

"Boy, this day just couldn't get any better. How does a stint in jail sound to you?" I whispered to my partner in crime.

Want me to lick his hand? Cooper offered, no doubt willing to do his part to defuse the situation.

"I want you to disappear," I said, feeling the chill of a dark cloud descending over us.

The sun visor was down, and a quick glance into the mirror confirmed I looked like someone who might try to skirt the law. My face was flushed in an unattractive shade of convict red, and sweat ran from my hairline.

Cooper was lounging on the steering wheel when a middle-aged, heavyset officer reached the driver's side window and tapped on it. He leaned over and slid Ray-Bans to the end of his bulbous nose. I opened the window as far as I dared, and Cooper dangled on the edge of it by his front paws before I could manifest what had happened. He gazed innocently at the policeman, and I heard *I'm charming him.*

"License and registration."

It's usually a good sign when they smile, I tried to convince myself. I fumbled inside the glove compartment to find the registration and dropped my wallet twice before I could produce my license. He checked both and eyed the damaged carrier.

"Officer, I've had the worst day," I huffed.

"I can see that," he said. "But it's no excuse for letting the cat drive." His generous belly shook with raucous laughter, and he lumbered to his patrol car.

I turned to Cooper. "He's probably calling his buddies at the precinct to tell them he's sitting behind a nut case whose cat was driving her home."

The officer returned with my ID and slid it through the small opening I provided. "I'd open the window wider, but Cooper can slide through the eye of a needle."

"This is the first ticket I've written for a cat driving without a license." He chuckled to himself. "What happened with the carrier?"

"Cooper freaked out when we were going through the car wash and chewed his way out of the box."

"You took your cat through a car wash?" He slapped his thighs and roared.

"Not initially. We went to the vet, and the car wash was on our way home," I said, realizing there was no rational explanation for what I had done.

The officer reached back and gave his trousers a tug. "I'll let this one slide. I'm pretty sure this is the last time I'll see your cat behind the wheel, and the two of you just gave me the best laugh I've had in years."

"Thank you, officer."

"We still have the problem of getting you home safely when your little buddy there seems determined to drive."

"I'll tie him to the passenger seat if I have to," I said, glaring at the offender. "My house is only two blocks away." Cooper settled into my lap, and I hoped he was as exhausted by our ordeal as I was and would stay put.

"I'll follow you," the nice policeman said, traipsing back to his car.

With "Officer Friendly" behind me, I carefully observed the speed limit of 35 mph. I wanted to slam my foot down on the accelerator and get into the garage before my wayward cat had another brainstorm. He seemed to sense the precarious nature of our situation and behaved accordingly. Finally at home and relatively unscathed, I lifted Cooper into my arms and felt the rumble of his contented purr.

Cooper's Rule:
Teach your mom that hogties
are for cattle.

Chapter 9   **TIES THAT BIND**

I baked a bad idea seasoned with good intentions. It's difficult to fire on all cylinders when you live with an uncontrollable cat like Cooper.

At the time, teaching him to walk on a harness didn't seem completely unreasonable. I purchased a handsome contraption for him and left it on the floor of my home office. Once he was used to the sight and scent of it, we could move to phase two. He sniffed it once or twice but basically found it boring. If it was in his way, he kicked it aside. Since Cooper was so unintimidated by the harness, it was time to saddle him up.

Hearing my footsteps padding toward him, an ear was already cocked in my direction when I entered the home office. We stood for a moment gazing at each other. I'll admit to being a bit apprehensive about the battle I anticipated. Cooper was intuitive enough to figure his mom was hatching a harebrained idea that involved his participation.

"Hey, buddy," I cooed. "What do you have planned right now?"

The sun God cast a beam on the chair. I'm going to dream in its warm glow, his sleepy eyes replied.

"But…"

The world will cease to exist for the next two hours. An aggressive yawn punctuated his expression.

"I have an idea," I offered, a tremble in my voice.

I'm familiar with your ideas. I'll pass. He licked a paw and turned toward the chair.

"This will be fun."

Like cramming me inside a small box and driving through a monsoon filled with ravenous predators? He hammered his point home with a sharp flick of his tail.

"I'll admit that wasn't a stellar moment."

I rest my case. Clearly he was anxious to end my tomfoolery and get on with his nap.

The screen door was closed so he couldn't escape before I had him trussed and ready for a walk. The battle of wills began.

Casually approaching him with the harness, I folded Cooper into my arms for a hug, then gently placed him on the desk chair and began to lace him into the harness. He was fully alert now and questioning my sanity.

What the? he clearly articulated while stiffening every appendage. His fur stood at attention, and he completely freaked out. Cooper flipped on his back like a calf before branding and began to spin like a top. I couldn't keep hold of him. The harness dangled from his thigh, when he burst through the screen door. He looked like an Irishman dancing a jig the way he shook his leg and kicked at the gadget arresting his flight. While he was engaged in a scuffle with the harness, I retrieved the screen door from the floor of my deck and placed it back on its track.

Cooper sputtered and spat. Profanities were tucked in a language

I was happy I couldn't understand. Finally free from the monster entangling him, my slightly deranged boy fled the premises. It was hours before I glimpsed his little face through the slider. When I opened it to apologize, he was reticent about coming too close to me again.

"See, Coop," I said, feeling like an abuser. "Nothing here to bind you." Odd the way my cat made me the guilty party whenever we differed. I opened the screen door. Cooper's eyes scanned every inch of my home office. When he felt certain nothing resembling restraints appeared anywhere in the room, he stepped across the threshold.

"I only wanted to protect you. Mom thought if you could learn to walk on a harness, we'd be able to enjoy time together outside, and you'd be safe."

Oh, yeah? I heard. *Did you plan to leap into trees with me and race across rooftops, because that's what I do?*

He had a point. I couldn't think of a way to counter it.

> **Cooper's Rule:**
> Before executing a dastardly act,
> make sure a sibling is nearby to
> assume the blame.

Chapter 10   RIDING THE CHRISTMAS TREE

Fall being the preamble to winter, I began to formulate a game plan for the long months Cooper would have to spend mostly inside. My focus was to redirect his rambunctious energy in order to minimize the damage to our home. Oh, he'd still frolic outside because weather was never a deterrent. But when temps hovered at zero and dropped below, his toes wouldn't be acclimated to more than a few minutes on frozen snow.

Coop did his part to help me rake the last of autumn's leaves, batting a few toward the opening in the leaf bags. And when those first downy flakes of snow arrived, he loped to the deck to greet them and licked the new season off his thickening coat. The brisk air fueled his body for speed and he tore through the house, bounding onto furniture and bouncing off walls. He and Chloe chased each other full-speed through every room as if a demon rode their tails.

I fought against a laser toy, at first feeling it was cruel to frustrate a cat that could never catch its prey. After figuring out a way to give them the illusion of capture, I succumbed and bought one; it was a fortuitous investment. I herded my cats throughout the house with this little red dot. They galloped like wild horses from room-to-room, paws thundering in pursuit of the illusive prey. From the bed to the wall, Cooper was airborne- slapping, pouncing and jumping, while Chloe waited her turn.

In quieter moments, I allowed the dot to rest on a paw, where they could at least touch it. But it was when I shone the red beam on a snow-covered back yard that the game kicked into high gear. The beam led them out onto the deck and down the stairs. Then it circled the yard, followed by two crazed and deliriously happy cats. They raced over the top of each other to see who could pounce on the red beast first. Their fervor stirred up powder and melded a feline version of snow angels into the yard. We spent many hours throughout the winter at this game and wore down a fair number of batteries.

At bedtime two properly worn out kitties, ready for a full night's sleep, joined me. It was around this time that Cooper decided to explore the dark caverns under the covers. I tented my legs, and he tunneled underneath the top sheet and blankets to stretch out between my ankles. Reading in bed, where it's quiet and comfortable, has always been my favorite way to wind down the day. While I read, Coop snoozed. Sometimes he surprised me with a little love bite on my ankle or heel. Within minutes he was snoring softly. When our combined body heat overwhelmed him, Cooper shot out of the covers like a rubber band and settled beside my right leg, or splayed out on his back on my thighs for as long as I could bear his weight.

I purchased a three-foot Christmas tree and displayed it on a plant stand in a corner of the living room. I added a billowy green tablecloth that reached the floor and secured it to the table with a red and gold ribbon; presentation is everything. I felt confident Chloe would admire the tree from a respectable distance. Cooper was the variable.

Years earlier, when I put up a five-foot tree in my Seattle condo, some of the horrors of *cat vs.Christmas tree* caught up with me. Sasha and CoCo climbed every branch. They gnawed or kicked off any decoration that got in their way. Returning home from work each day, I was greeted by some new form of destruction. The tree came down before Christmas and two grieving cats never completely forgave me, as they watched their favorite toy being dismantled and boxed up forever.

I realized the chance I took with Cooper, but because the tree was small and displayed on a table, it would probably be safe. The little guy often draped himself across the back of the loveseat and gazed into the tree. He probably compared it to his favorite evergreen in the back yard and wondered why no birds sought the shelter of its branches.

A few days before Christmas, presents arrived from my friend, Carolyn, in Seattle. I opened the cardboard box to place them under the tree. Carolyn, who always wraps gifts in unique packaging, had clipped a sparkling gold and white bird to one of my gift boxes. It was meant to be an ornament. I found the perfect spot for it next to a gold light that illuminated the bird to perfection.

One evening my feline family and I were all a bit drowsy. I was stretched out in the glider watching a mind-numbing re-run of a Hallmark Christmas movie, Chloe lay half-asleep on the floor near the tree, and Cooper was sprawled on top of the loveseat across from the tree gazing into the lights. Slowly, the mood in the room changed. Coop's eyes performed a bored drift across the branches. They stopped abruptly when, for the first time, he spotted the bird. I wasn't overly concerned, even when his tail lashed from side-to-side and thumped against the loveseat. After all, the bird didn't have a pulse. It wasn't moving, or breathing, or tweeting a tune to draw his interest. I knew he'd figure it out soon, and indifference would prevail. Still . . . a fixed stare on Cooper typically meant that a diabolical idea was fomenting in his agile brain. In a flash, he was up on his twinkle toes. He danced back and forth on the back of the loveseat, assessing the best angle for attack.

He was already airborne by the time I sputtered, "NO-O-O!" I tripped over my own feet attempting to rise off the glider. He slammed against the tree, and gripped it with all fours, as if he were riding a bull. Together, they toppled to the floor. At first he just laid on the tree, seemingly shocked it hadn't withstood the weight of his assault. He glanced at Chloe, who'd dashed into the dining room to avoid a collision.

"Don't look at her," I accused. "You're the one riding the tree."

By now he figured things looked bad for him. He grabbed the bird in his teeth and took off for parts unknown. A day later, a thorough search uncovered the bird lying under the mirrored vanity in my bedroom. A few puncture wounds marred the shiny surface of its body.

Cooper's excuse: *I wanted to see what sparkle tasted like.*

My query: "And?"

The result of Cooper's taste test: *Pooh!*

Cooper's Rule:
When all else fails, cop a plea.

Chapter 11   CABIN FEVER

After the debacle with the Christmas tree, Cooper kept a low profile for a few days. That seemed to be the maximum amount of time he could manage to stay out of trouble. Being inside for most of the day and bored to tears, he invented new ways in which to amuse himself at the expense of me or my home.

Chloe never jumped up on the dining room table. I didn't allow Cooper on the dining room table. This meant nothing to him, as he didn't recognize rules or barriers. We often played a game of wills when it came to surfaces upon which food was placed. From my glider, I could see half the table through the archway between the living room and dining room. If the plant in the center of the table began to shimmy, it meant a restless marauder was up there giving it a trim.

"Get off the table, Cooper." The plant shook with a vengeance. "Don't make me get up from my chair." Of course he made me get up from my chair. It gave him a kick to wait and see if I'd actually come after him. Then he gambled I'd get within grabbing distance before he bothered to jump down. This was a scenario that played to conclusion on most nights.

Cooper trimmed all my plants with his razor-sharp teeth. When I objected to having them desecrated in such a manner, he frowned as if to say, *I sculpt them. A connoisseur of art would recognize the difference.* He shamed me further by continuing. *I perform this service at no cost. You would have to pay a professional a premium to achieve a less attractive result.*

While "sculpting" he often pulled out a palm frond or two and enlisted the willowy lengths as toys. He tossed them into the air or slid them along the hardwood floors in the dining room. He could fashion anything into a source of gayety. He was not above dragging amputated fronds across the top of my couch or loveseat and leaving them there. He preferred the "rugged" look and found great sport in repurposing my furniture and accessories. I have yet to find a sachet he stole off my mirrored vanity while I slept.

One morning, desperately in need of caffeine to pry my eyes open, I tramped into the kitchen and found Cooper lounging on the counter, where he knew he shouldn't be. There's a metal wine glass holder under one of my cupboards. It houses a couple of Princess House champagne flutes and six Waterford Crystal wine goblets. Cooper was directly underneath. I froze. Any sudden movement from me might encourage him to stand up and flee. If he rose, he'd shatter the goblets, not to mention the damage an explosion of glass could do to his head. His wispy eyebrows met in the middle of his forehead, and I saw him form the question, *I'm on the counter…how come you're not yelling?*

"How 'bout a nice back scratch for my favorite boy?" I said in a sugary mom voice, cautiously approaching him. Scratching his back and cooing, I slid him out of harm's way and thanked Jesus for freezing him in place.

When I swung him away from the counter to put him on the

floor, his foot caught inside the handle of my Capresso coffee pot and swept it across the kitchen. It crashed into pieces on the floor. The commotion summoned Chloe. I shouted for her to stay away and lunged over glass with Cooper in my arms. Then I loped out of the kitchen with all the grace of Quasimodo to contain both cats in the safety of my office until the mess could be cleaned up. When drops of blood followed, I knew I hadn't jumped far enough. I no longer needed caffeine to open my eyes, adrenaline had done the trick. My cats survived the shards, but their mom spent the better part of the morning cleaning up debris and doctoring a bloody foot.

My bundle of joy continued to find inappropriate ways of entertaining himself while I prayed for spring and freedom for all of us. My water bill spiked when he took a fancy to flushing the toilet in order to watch the torrent of bubbling water disappear down the drain. I quickly closed the lid on that activity.

One afternoon he surprised me in the shower ala *Psycho*, when his shadow gradually rose against the plastic liner. I dropped the soap and while bending to retrieve it, my elbow grazed the shower curtain. Canines pierced through the liner like a knife slicing through flesh. I recoiled in fear and nearly lost my footing. A shoulder butted the shower liner aside, and Cooper's face greeted me. *Scared ya, didn't I?* his sly smile suggested. He watched warm water splash against tile and was calm for a moment, calculating. Then he hopped into the tub and batted at droplets until he was waterlogged and ready to try something new.

On too many occasions, he appropriated *my* bathroom sink for a napping place at the exact moment I needed to use it. I swear he read my thoughts and planted himself accordingly.

"Move, Coop," I pleaded. He quickly adopted an *I don't think so* attitude. As soon as I began to lift him, his body went slack, and he mouthed, *Go ahead, make my day.*

His cabin fever truly tested my patience. "I know a guy named Guido who'll take you for a long walk off a short pier," I threatened, to no avail. Most of the warnings in my arsenal made his little tummy cramp with laughter. Only one put the starch in his fur. It went something like this. "Hey, Coop, I've been reading up on taxidermy." The "T" word sent him underground. Or, the cat equivalent; he started hiding under my throw rugs. When I noticed the rug in front of the entry door had grown a tail, I leaned over and tapped the lump above it. Coop's eyes peeked out from a corner. At first I thought it was fear that sent him into hiding, but he'd just discovered a new game. When Chloe joined him under the rug, Cooper tried to convince me she was the one terrorized by the taxidermy threat. I assured him she was never part of the equation.

"You need to bank some good deeds, little fella," I told him.

***

My first duty after a snowfall was to clear a path on the deck for the little prince. When he had a trail to follow, he'd prance to the giant snowbank of accumulated drift and wait for me to grab a handful of snow and mold a snowball. I'd toss it high into the air and Cooper would leap up and slam it into oblivion with his paw. He slapped those snowballs until I grew weary of fashioning them. My boy often "guilted" me into continuing the game long after I was ready to return to a warm house. He'd sit on his tushy and elongate his face until the whites of his eyes were prominent, and he appeared sufficiently forlorn.

The little man often coerced me into opening the front storm door to show him the *evidence* for keeping him inside. On one such occasion, while thick feathery flakes piled into inches, Cooper slipped outside and bounced down the four front steps to the walkway, where he sat in the silent night. Snow danced like fairies on his body, slowly enveloping him in a frosty blanket from his haunches to his shoulders. I watched him sit as still as a statue, his little form disappearing into the pearly landscape. When Cooper was certain no creatures were stirring, he rose, shook off velvety snow, and trotted back inside. A taste was all he'd needed.

Cooper's Rule:
If there's too much estrogen in
your house, dilute with catnip.

Chapter 12   DYSLEXIA AND THE LITTER BOX

Cooper and Chloe often played in the basement where they had wide, open spaces in which to pursue each other, and a heap of storage boxes to investigate. During some adventure, Cooper must have bonked his head. But instead of amnesia, he experienced temporary dyslexia.

I wouldn't have believed it if I hadn't seen it with my own eyes. Apparently, Cooper felt nature's call at the same time I took laundry to the basement. Both litter boxes are downstairs, and I pass them on my way to the laundry room. Coop entered his Booda Dome front first and stopped halfway in. He looked so funny I laughed. I stopped laughing when the working end dumped poops and peeps on the tile floor.

"Cooper, you're doing it backwards," I said. By the time I got over to assist the rest of him inside the box, he was finished, and I had a mess to clean up. For some reason I'll never understand, this behavior continued for about two days. Then he seemed to figure it out again and didn't leave me anymore unwelcome surprises.

***

Chloe enjoyed an occasional roll in catnip, but Cooper was a major addict. I walked into my office one afternoon to find him steeped in leaves. He was surrounded by every toy I had either bought my cats or made for them that had the slightest whiff of catnip in it; they were all eviscerated. The man of the house was mellowing out on his back, his furry face covered in drool.

"Cooper, I'm gonna have to vacuum for days to get all this crap up."

His eyes rolled in my general direction, and all I heard was *Ah-h-h-h-h*.

***

Winter was wearing thin on my boy and me. Chloe was the only member of the family who took Cooper's shenanigans and my subsequent hysteria in stride. She was beside me in the kitchen when the banging in the basement began. I was washing a load of laundry and since Cooper was nowhere to be seen, I assumed he was the source of the noise. Chloe chose to let me conduct the investigation on my own.

"Coop? Are you down here?" I called, stepping into the basement.

Bang!…Bang!….Bang!

Metal crashing against metal reverberated through my fillings and my teeth hurt. I picked up the pace to the laundry room. A little rascal sat on top of the washing machine. He opened the lid and watched it slam back into place. I assumed he amused himself by examining the agitating motion of laundry and couldn't figure out how to make the lid stay open.

Note to self: Find a heavy object to keep the lid closed.

My face crumpled into the scariest frown I could muster. "Really, Coop? The washing machine? You could have fallen in and drowned."

He raised a paw, then licked it and smoothed back his whiskers, acting bored by my concern. I wasn't certain whether he was exhibiting shame or defiance. Knowing Coop, it was his way of flipping me off.

I picked up the little villain and planted him on my shoulder for the ride upstairs.

> Cooper's Rule:
> When your mom catches you
> doing something naughty,
> shake your booty.

Chapter 13 SPRING RULES, WINTER DROOLS

When spring finally arrived, Cooper and I heard a chorus of angels sing; it was joined by the popping sound of our bonds releasing us from the frozen tundra. I opened the front door to breathe in the season, and Coop shot through my legs and disappeared...for twenty-four horrendous hours!

I assumed my recurring role as tortured mom, scouting the neighborhood in search of her headstrong son. Sleep was a luxury not meant for me, and I beat every bush to find my boy. When I made my way home, exhausted and defeated, the prodigal son was waiting for me on the deck. My plan to throttle him within an inch of his life melted away. I picked him up and hugged him so tight to my chest, that my pounding heartbeat spanked him vigorously.

"Cooper, you are going to be the death of me," I mumbled into his fragrant fur.

He knew when to keep his mouth shut and purr like a son-of-a-gun.

The next afternoon, while we were on the deck, Coop introduced me to his "happy dance." First, he made sure he had my eye, then he ran into the grass, flopped onto his back and did a little jig.

Immediately, I began to sing, *Shake, shake, shake: shake, shake, shake: shake your booty, shake your booty.* These lyrics were all I could remember of the 1976 KC and the Sunshine Band ditty. Coop seemed to appreciate the musical accompaniment because he shook to the rhythm of the song. Harmony returned to our lives…for a while.

A couple days later, I was backing out of my driveway to run some errands when I noticed a man in a Toyota Camry hit his brakes hard and gesture for me to roll down my window. I stopped and followed his lead.

"Lady, there's a cat on the roof of your car."

Oh, let me guess. I felt my blood pressure spike, as I opened the door and pulled myself out of the car. I waved to the stranger. "Thanks." He drove off.

Cooper sat on his haunches and blinked at me.

"What were you thinking?" I sputtered.

He lowered his head, and I heard, *Well…you won't let me drive.*

"I thought you were inside napping."

I reached for him, but he anticipated my move and sprang onto the front lawn. Assessing my mood, he fled.

Cooper's Rule:
If your mom has a soft heart,
take full advantage.

Chapter 14 HANGIN' WITH THE FERALS AND THE COONS

I've known my share of heartache over the years, caring for feral cats who traipsed onto my property looking disheveled and hungry. The first was a mother and her kitten. They looked like they'd fought the ten-day war and lost. The minute I saw them, I produced food and water. The two appeared sick and starved to the bone. I couldn't get near, so observed them for a couple days. Mother and baby must have fallen victim to nature's version of the Grim Reaper. Still, they had time to spread the word because the pilgrimage to my back yard began.

I moved an Adirondack loveseat from my deck to the garage and made it cozy with old towels, a furry cushion and plenty of fleece blankets. In winter, I placed hand warmers under the blankets to add a little comfort when the kitties cuddled together at night to ward off below zero temperatures. Added to the décor were a placemat, plastic food bowls, and an electric water bowl that plugged into an outlet in the garage to keep their drinking water from freezing when temps plummeted. Knowing there were bound to be a few drug addicts among them, I made a couple of catnip socks for the ferals to drool on. The access door to my garage was always cracked open so the cats could come and go at will. The only thing lacking was a sign above the door that read *Feral Cat B&B*. From time-to-time a few unwelcome guests also partook of the largess in my garage. On more than one occasion I was surprised by a neighborhood skunk or raccoon.

Cooper seemed to have a magic potion that allowed him to interact with both feral cats and raccoons without incident. Maybe the ferals were a part of his "hood" but I couldn't explain the raccoons; they kill cats. You can imagine my horror when I checked the deck one afternoon to find Cooper entertaining a couple of small raccoons. I knew Chloe was under her tree bird watching and probably unaware of Cooper's play date with the killer coons. I shuddered at the thought of her wandering back to the deck unaware.

Opening the slider with caution, I called out to the visiting beasts. "Go home."

They both acknowledged my presence with a nod but seemed unintimidated and disinclined to leave the party.

I didn't have a manual that detailed a safe way to be forceful without initiating a skirmish. I slid the screen door open and deepened my voice as close to an alto as I could muster. "Go away!" I added the requisite rude gesture, flicking my hands in their direction.

The wild beasts finally got the message, but they took their sweet time moseying down the steps of my deck. I watched them waddle across the grass and scurry under the fence.

I turned my attention to Cooper. He seemed dumbstruck by my rudeness in calling an end to the festivities before the DJ arrived. "No more raccoon parties on the deck, Coop." He snorted, and I heard *What a buzz kill.*

***

I tried not to form an emotional attachment with the feral cats but when you watch kittens play in your back yard and grow over time, the familiar sight of them begins to soften your heart.

My endeavor to help the ferals wasn't always successful. I shed my share of tears after finding kittens killed by wild things or retrieving cats who'd been hit by cars in front of my house.

Allow me to stand on my soapbox for a moment and offer a plea to all pet owners to spay and neuter their animals. My wish is for everyone with an unwanted pet to take them to their local Humane Society. They'll be fed, housed and well cared for, and they'll have a chance of finding a forever home. Animals who are dumped, and their offspring, lead short, miserable lives. And those of us who love them are left to pick up the pieces. Our hearts are shredded in the process.

The longest period of time I saw the same ferals come and go from my garage was two years. I don't know if that was their total lifespan or if they had simply found better digs. The sad truth is that there was always another to fill their place. None were confrontational but all were skittish and never approached the house. That was about to change.

Cooper's Rule:
If you spot tears on your
mom's cheeks, lick them off.

Chapter 15   CARLY'S STORY

I broke my own rule when a couple of feral kittens engaged with my cats and me. I named them. The gray and white female sporting a heart-shaped pink nose, became Carly. She quickly fell in love with Cooper and shadowed him all over the yard. If you look closely at the picture in the previous chapter, you'll see her crouched on the deck railing bird watching with the man of her heart.

Carly's steel-gray brother, a bit more standoffish, was Connor. These were the only two kittens in a litter of five who showed an interest in a scary human. They took tentative steps onto the deck for special treats like tuna and salmon. After months of socializing, Carly allowed me to pet her. This was a feral kitten who really wanted a home, and I was falling in love with her. Connor became fairly socialized but was still skittish in a way Carly never was. She was sweetness in a small package, and trust shone purely in her eyes.

Just as little brothers and sisters are often deemed pests by their older siblings, sometimes Cooper found their presence annoying. He took that opportunity to smack one or both of them out of his way. Whoever had been targeted would fall on their back in complete submission. Neither feral ever showed any sign of aggression. They were perfectly happy to acknowledge Cooper as their leader in order to remain in his kingdom. My boy cemented their allegiance with his own brand of coercion. I often heard him admonishing his new followers to *watch and learn*.

I constructed a little tent on the deck for the two ferals, since they preferred being close to the house. It included warm beds and food and water. They slept inside the tent, rather than in the garage with their siblings. Much as Carly adored Cooper, and fancied herself his future bride, she didn't follow him on his excursions if it meant venturing too far from the security of our back yard.

Carly and Connor scooted inside on occasion but didn't wander far from their escape hatch, the slider to the deck. I found it amazing that Cooper tolerated their presence in his home. They probably didn't stay long enough to try his patience.

Carly and I participated in an affectionate ritual before she hunkered down in her tent. Each night, while I performed my ablutions before bedtime, she vaulted onto the corner of the deck railing next to my bathroom window. Once she had my attention, Carly rubbed her face against the glass. I sent her air kisses. She waited until I lowered the Roman curtain to jump down and snuggle up with Connor in their beds.

Our harmonious arrangement with these special feral kittens continued for nearly a year. I must not have noticed the gradual exit of their siblings. When Connor disappeared, I felt desperate and kept a keen eye on Carly. The night after Connor went missing, I made a bed for Carly in my office. I let her out on the deck early the next morning and never saw her again. When she didn't appear to eat her wet food treat and failed to answer my frantic calls, I was heartsick.

I spoke with some of my neighbors and learned the ferals had wandered into the driveway of a nearby neighbor. She trapped them all with tempting food treats over a four-day period and took them to the Humane Society. My stomach twisted into a knot because their policy was to immediately euthanize feral cats. I knew there wasn't any hope for Conner, but I was able to get in touch with them the day Carly vanished. They were closing, and a verbal description wasn't helpful enough.

The next morning I broke a few rules of the road to get to the Humane Society with Carly's picture, hoping to identify her. They allowed my search of their holding area since I was so desperate to find her. She had already been dispatched. This shook me to my core. I made myself sick sobbing over the feral kittens, but Carly, in particular. All she wanted was a home and once she found one, she was ripped away so egregiously.

Cooper's Rule:
If your mom locks you inside,
teach her it's a bad idea.

Chapter 16   **REVENGE**

I was about to turn my house over to two cats for a couple of days. A friend invited me to her family's cottage on the water up north near Rhinelander, and I needed a change of scene after recent events with the feral cats.

It would drive my boy crazy to be sequestered inside for over 48 hours. He was bound to peer out a window and lock eyes with a mouse that he could turn into a spinning top. He'd resent me for shackling his body when his imagination was so ripe. I envisioned him sprinting through every room in search of a doorway to wonderland and deconstructing my home in the process.

I made him a fresh catnip sock, hoping he'd slip into a drugged stupor that would mitigate the damage. Leaving him on his own in the house was a bit like giving the car keys to a twelve-year-old and tossing in a six-pack of Coors.

I gathered my children around me, but the message was for the rowdy one.

"Coop, Mom's taking a much-deserved sabbatical. I won't be gone long, and I trust you to keep a low profile. Before you 're-arrange' anything, ask yourself this question: What would Jesus do?"

His face was blank, but I knew he was already plotting revenge.

"If you need to hunt, look for bugs. The only work I require of you and Chloe is to keep bugs out of sight."

Day one by the lake was as relaxing as a visit to a spa. By the second day away, I was already dreading the inevitable. My house had been cat-proofed. Still, plants were always vulnerable, and Cooper had a penchant for hiding my belongings.

Thirty minutes from home, my palms leaked sweat and itchy arms begged to be scratched. By the time I reached the driveway, my pulse had quickened and breathing was difficult. Cooper watched my arrival from a front window. The light wasn't good enough for me to gage the level of guilt on his face. His body language was to be a barometer of the destruction awaiting me inside. My hand actually shook, and I struggled to get the key in the lock. When the front door opened, Cooper shot between my legs and found freedom.

"Not even a hello?" I asked the orange blur that blasted across my grass.

I hadn't looked inside yet. When I stepped into the foyer, my eyes rolled around the living room, assessing the mess. Chloe snaked her body through my legs, braiding her fur into my cotton pedal-pushers and purred a hello. At least someone was happy to see me.

"No wonder the culprit fled," I said to her. "It looks like the Feds were here and tossed the place in a drug bust." Sofa pillows were an explosion of color across the living room floor; to Cooper they were just soft hockey pucks. The Pier 1 pillar candles, that formerly graced my coffee table, had been knocked to the floor and were sprawled in every direction. Cooper left his sister to face the music alone. She was plastered to a corner of the loveseat monitoring my reaction to her brother's renovation.

"Were you guys ballroom dancing on my coffee table?" I asked Chloe. She closed her eyes and feigned a nap. Cooper had obviously tortured a vow of silence from her. "I'm gonna need a stiff drink to carry me through the rest of the house."

At first glance, the dining room appeared untainted…except for the plant that Cooper loved to shimmy with; he'd given it a crew cut.

On the way to my office, I stopped and backed into the kitchen. Something was different. I looked up. *Oh, jeez.* The scoundrel had been on top of the refrigerator. B.C. (before Cooper) a decorative basket was the centerpiece on top. I filled it with hydrangeas collected from my bushes on either side of the front porch. As their colors changed with the seasons, from green to white to rust, I gathered the blooms and created a varied dried arrangement. Cooper reduced it to several inches of colorful dust. Flower parts had emigrated to the inside of the refrigerator. The largest portion of debris found a home in the corner of the floor next to the fridge.

I ventured into my home office, which also served as my cats' play room. In Cooper's mind, the shared space granted him liberty to add his own personal touch. In this instance, demolition won the day. A four-legged tornado had blown through the room, re-distributing every sheet of paper and small object that wasn't weighed down. I found tablets and printer paper under my desk, file cabinets, and bookshelf. I'm not sure how he managed to wedge sheets of paper into corners of the sliding glass door, but partially chewed sheets were front and center. Books were strewn across the floor, and framed pictures on the bookshelf were toppled in every direction. Miraculously, my plants were still upright. But Cooper must have played in the dirt, then walked across my printer, leaving faint impressions of his wickedness.

"Your brother is so grounded," I shouted to Chloe.

Standing at my bedroom door, I wished for a distillery in the basement that could cook up some good old-fashioned prohibition whiskey. That's what I needed to face the enormous regurgitated fur ball (fresh and still glistening) on my rose petal pillow. And then there was my bed...so violated. It looked like Caligula and his friends had spent the weekend having an orgy on it. My decorative pillows were mashed and smooshed, their original purpose barely recognizable. Enumerable body forms were pressed into vivid shapes on my once-pristine blue-and-white quilt; a thin layer of fur was the overlay. Suffice it to say, I spent the next two hours restoring my home to its former state.

Cooper would have some splainin' to do. I didn't expect to see him again until the wee small hours. And by that time, he knew there'd be no evidence linking him to the mischief.

> Cooper's Rule:
> If a death occurs while you're
> engaged in play, flee the scene
> until your accomplice removes
> the evidence.

Chapter 17   MY CAT, THE SERIAL KILLER

I couldn't put it off any longer. Weeds were winning the war in my flower beds. My poor lilies screamed for attention. Stepping off the deck, I was soon confronted with a bloated dead body. No. Every fiber of my being rejected the idea of a giant rat, but the ropey tail confirmed its identity. All that stood between me and a cadaver were a pair of cotton gardening gloves. *I can do this. I'm small but flinty.*

Steeling myself to touch a rotting kill, I bent over, grasped the long tail, and swung the animal to eye level. I kept it as far from my face as possible while inspecting the body. Without an autopsy, it was impossible to determine the cause of death. There were no visible puncture wounds or blood. For obvious reasons, I don't use poisons in my yard. Cooper was known to play with his prey until they expired – no doubt from fright. Can a rat die of cardiac arrest?

It felt like I was taking a perp walk to the end of my back yard, the eyes of the neighborhood upon me. After a guilty glance in every direction, I tossed the corpse over my fence and into the alley beyond. Unless one of my neighbors was equipped with a telescope, no one saw me dispose of the evidence.

Walking to my flower beds, I stepped on something soft and mushy; it was another carcass. This one was mostly decayed, but the ears and fur qualified it as a rabbit. I strolled the perimeter of my house, counting bodies as I went. There were a total of six: the initial rat, one rabbit, two squirrels, a chipmunk and a mouse. All were in various stages of decomposition. Cooper had turned my previously untainted yard into the equivalent of an FBI body farm. Was my cat a serial killer?

I turned in a half-circle, hoping to spot the perpetrator. "Coo-per! Coo-per?"

Of course, he was nowhere to be seen. He probably glimpsed my gardening attire and flew the coop. I surreptitiously disposed of the remaining carcasses in the same manner, and in the same hiding place, the alley. Cooper had just made his mother an accessory after the fact.

An hour later, I was adding fresh mulch to the base of my split birch tree in the front yard. Glancing up the street, I noticed Cooper prancing down the sidewalk with two kitties in tow. I watched them trot down the driveway toward the garage and called to my boy.

"Don't bring home any new mouths for me to feed. I'm already nourishing a clowder of feral cats, plus half the wild kingdom."

He puffed out his chest, as if to say *I'm a chick magnet. Get used to it.*

"Did you tell your girlfriends they're partying with a serial killer? We need to talk."

After Cooper finished entertaining his ladies and I had completed my gardening chores, I confronted him about the victims he left strewn over the yard. The best place for me to lay down the law with my errant boy was at his food bowl while he scarfed down his meal.

"Do not leave fresh or decomposing carcasses in plain view all over the yard for your mother to dispose of. Got that?"

I stood behind Cooper blowing fury at him. The best he could give me were two ears cocked in my direction.

"Well?" I was determined to get a response.

He stopped eating but didn't turn his head to address me. I heard, *Aliens left those bodies in the yard.*

"Aliens? Where did you get that idea?"

We watched The X Files *the other night. Aliens kill things and blame cats* was his argument.

Clearly, I had lost my grip. Intimidation rolled off his back like a summer rain. Where did I go wrong? It was my mission to convince him I was the alpha member of our little family. Rules would be set, and he would comply. I would learn this was a misconceived idea.

Cooper's Rule:
Cats don't do dog tricks.
We have our own.

Chapter 18   TRICKS FOR TREATS?

Cooper, being the intellectual giant I knew him to be, would probably enjoy learning some tricks. The interaction would be fun for both of us, and the experience would be a positive way to direct his energy and re-establish some boundaries. Granted, I would need to keep him inside and focused on the task. So naturally I chose to approach him after a nap. He always woke slowly and with a sunny disposition. I would take full advantage of his good humor.

Armed with a can of Friskies Savory Shreds with Chicken and Gravy, I waited for Cooper to return from slumber land. His eyelids flickered and opened. Since it was uncommon for me to loom over him when he woke, he looked duly surprised.

"Hey, buddy," I began in an encouraging voice. "Want to learn to shake hands and roll over?"

He yawned, and I heard, *What? So I'm a dog now?*

Coop rose from the glider, where he'd been dozing, and glanced toward the front windows. I'm sure the little man was anxious to get back outside where the action was. He sniffed in the direction of the open can of cat food, and pushed his tushy into a peak. Then he reached forward and gave his front legs a good long stretch. I heard the sweet rumble of his purr and kissed the top of his head. He slid to the floor and sat. Always observing good table manners, Coop cleaned his front paws with his tongue in preparation for a snack.

I sat beside my boy, crossed my legs in the lotus position, and offered him a taste of his treat from a spoon. While he savored a bit of gravy, I took hold of his left paw and gently shook it. "Shake hands," I said at the same time. He looked at me like I'd just grown a second head, and slowly pulled his paw free. While he took another lick of gravy, I repeated the action and command. He repeated his rejection.

"This is something fun we can do together, Coop. Believe me, it impresses the heck out of people at parties."

He snorted, and I heard, *I had more fun watching cement dry.*

"Let's try a couple more times." If I couldn't get him to shake hands, what would he do when I rolled him over?

He shook his head and took a step back, as if to say, *I don't do tricks for treats. Such antics are beneath my dignity.*

I continued giving him licks from the spoon, while taking his paw and issuing the command.

I could be chasing a squirrel across the roof right now, I heard, just before he bolted for the back door.

Okay, his attention span needed work. It was time to set the little varmint free. Maybe he'd be open to the idea of learning something new after a jaunt outside.

Cooper made a point of demonstrating how happy he was to be in the arms of Mother Nature. He bounded through the grass, then flopped onto his back and performed his happy dance. Since he preferred musical accompaniment, I found my key and sang the *Shake Your Booty* song for him. His funny little jig pressed a grass stain into his fur while the sun warmed his tummy. Chloe and I gazed upon our prince with all the love and admiration he felt entitled to.

A couple hours later, Cooper stopped back inside for a snack; a good time to resume his training. He licked his paws and studied me, quickly deducing his mother's scheme.

"Come here, Coop," I called, patting the area rug where I sat. He looked skeptical, but ambled into the living room anyway to appease me. Cats can be accommodating when they wish. I picked him up, careful to capture both his front and back paws in my hands. Then I laid him on his side and tried to roll him over with a "Roll over" command. His eyes folded into slits. I interpreted this expression to mean, *What the...? Have you lost your mind?* Then he figured it out. Mom wanted to see his happy dance. He rolled to his back and jiggled like his life depended on it. All I could do was laugh. I didn't have a clue how to train a cat. Under similar circumstances, I would have come to the same conclusion he did.

Both my cats hated having their paws touched, so the handshake idea was D.O.A. Trying to get Coop to roll over was clearly going to initiate a jig; another idea for the dust bin.

Cooper was a wild and crazy cat, and I wasn't going to change him. He was super smart and if I couldn't keep him sufficiently stimulated, he would find ways (mostly inappropriate) in which to incite his own imagination. I could forget rules and compliance when it came to Cooper. The greatest part of his charm was the fact he was so unpredictable. He was a free spirit and mulish as my boy often was, I wouldn't have changed a thing about him. I grudgingly gave up the battle. He was the alpha in our family.

Cooper's Rule:
Never bring your mom a gift
that runs toward her.

Chapter 19   A MOUSE IN THE HOUSE

I was in the midst of a blue menopausal moment. Guess I shouldn't have been reading about world events on the Internet. The thump of paws racing up the steps of my deck, shifted my attention to the cats about to make an appearance. The slider and screen were open for easy access.

Cooper stepped into my home office with live vermin in his mouth. A tail wagged to and fro as he walked. Chloe stood behind him, reverence shining in her eyes.

I had no idea a woman of my advanced age could move so quickly, but this situation was a crisis in progress.

"No! No! No! Back out of the house with that thing."

Cooper dropped the mouse on the carpet, and it immediately sprinted toward me. I wish to qualify my agitation by making it clear that I have no fear of "pet" mice or rats. Both have been quite friendly toward me in the past. However, this was a wild mouse that could carry disease. If it escaped inside my house, chances were good we'd have a permanent resident from that day forward.

The little mouse, no doubt frightened and confused, stopped. Perhaps it was trying to determine its next move, but that was just enough time for Cooper to scoop it up again. I did have the presence of mind to stumble to the office door and slam it shut. Neither cat, nor mouse, was going to leave the room if I could help it.

"Take that thing outside, Coop." My plan to hoist him out the door with the wild thing backfired. He identified this experience as the best game he'd come up with in a while. I went for the tackle. Like a running back, Coop cut to the left and dashed around me. He had the ball and was racing for a touchdown.

The stringy tail wagging from Cooper's mouth drove me crazy. His sly smile said *This is a toy we can both play with.* The little devil galloped around the room like a horse around a show ring. I stumbled behind him trying to shoo him out the slider. He dropped the mouse again, and I knew it was in shock. It was about a foot from freedom but didn't see its advantage. Coop crouched beside it and batted it into the air. I hustled to the closet door and snatched it open. Without much trouble, I found the plastic cup and sheet of cardboard used to trap insects for release outside. The cup would work for our tiny mouse.

"Out of the way, Coop," I shouted, reaching for the mouse. It must have gotten a shot of adrenaline because it darted under the bookcase.

"I feel a new stress wrinkle sprouting," I told the troublemaker.

Cup and cardboard at the ready, I knelt and peered under the bookcase. *I swear, cat and mouse are in cahoots.* The mouse was grooming its whiskers, as if it had an audition for Disney. Its only path to freedom was through the front of the bookcase. The back and both sides are flush with the carpet. I grabbed some books and blocked all but a small passageway out. Then I reached for the spray bottle of water employed to break up cat tussles and squirted it at the mouse. This nonsense was supposed to send it charging into the cup. But that would have been too easy. If I'd read my horoscope that day, I'm sure it would have warned: *Stay in bed, or all hell will break loose.*

I gazed at the mouse. The mouse gazed at me. Time to block the front of the bookcase completely and find a lure. I didn't think there was any cheese in the house. How cliché. Surely, one can catch a mouse with something besides cheese. Lettuce? Hum, that's more tempting to rabbits.

I dashed to the kitchen to check my fridge. *Oh, there's a cold hotdog.* There was more commotion in the office. I grabbed the hotdog and ran. Cooper must have pushed one of the books aside and snatched the mouse back. That infernal tail was wagging from his mouth again.

This time I had the element of surprise. Coop was focused on the hotdog. I scooped him into my arms and sprinted to the door. In my zeal to get the mouse away from my house, I stumbled down the steps of the deck and nearly fell. I dropped Cooper on the grass and hurried back inside.

It's anybody's guess what happened to it, but in this instance, I rooted for the mouse. All I can tell you is that its body didn't end up in *my* yard.

> Cooper's Rule:
> If you need to hide from your mom, fold yourself up like a pocketknife.

Chapter 20   **TRAVELIN' MAN**

About to leave for Rhinelander to perform some maintenance at our family gravesite, I wanted Cooper inside for the few hours I'd be away. No doubt he was helping Mother Nature prune the wildlife population. Calling him didn't bear fruit. I decided to make a quick trip to the dry cleaners to pick up a few items. He'd probably turn up for a snack before my departure.

Having completed my mission and about a mile from home, I glanced out the window of my car. An orange and white cat was bouncing down the sidewalk, tail reaching for the sky, and apparently happy as a clam. *Aw, cute kitty. He looks just like...Coop?* I drove a block ahead of the cat and pulled over to confirm my suspicion. *It is Cooper. What's he doing in a commercial district?*

As he approached the car, the little man noticed my head hanging out the window and stopped. The look of surprise on his face prompted a chuckle. I heard him say *Mom? What are you doing here?*

"You are so busted. You're nearly a mile from home. Get in the car." I opened my door.

Cooper looked at the open door, then back at me. I saw him weigh his options. He knew I wasn't happy, and I'd interrupted his carefree little jaunt.

"Come on, Coop," I cooed, patting the top of my thighs. He backed up a couple steps. Not the reaction I hoped for. Maybe he remembered all the drama of his last trip in the car. "No car wash this time. I promise." A few spectators smiled as they strode past. "Come on," I hissed. "This is embarrassing. We're drawing a crowd."

Cooper took a few tentative steps toward the car. He noticed the steering wheel and leapt into my lap. *Can I drive?* was the question that formed on his face.

"Would I look good in prison garb?"

He settled into my lap for the ride home. While Coop enjoyed the sights from my window, I kept a keen eye out for "Officer Friendly." My cat wasn't driving, but I knew the policeman wouldn't be happy to see Cooper outside his carrier a second time.

When we returned home, the little man followed me inside. His normal routine was to indulge in a snack, then find a comfy place to nap. I could find solace in knowing where he was and what he was doing for the next few hours.

***

The second floor in my 1935 Tudor home consists of a sitting area, two bedrooms and a bath. I use it as guest quarters and luckily, there's a door in the foyer that closes it off from the rest of the house. Upstairs is "Area 51" where my cats are concerned. You can imagine the machinations Cooper indulged in to sneak into any space where he knew he wasn't welcome.

He saw an opportunity while the door was open and my arms were loaded with cleaning supplies. My guardian angel had a hold of my elbow when Coop shot between my legs, or I'd have ended up a pile of bones at the bottom of the stairs. I swear I heard him snickering while he hid.

The chase began. There was no use calling him; he wouldn't answer. My boy always made me find him. As soon as I spotted a tail, a paw, or an ear, the little reprobate darted to a new hiding place. He lived for this game. Coop could expect to be the victor for at least 10 to 15 minutes. When my heat index reached the boiling point, the punk escaped back downstairs, chuckling all the way.

Another game Cooper delighted in was grabbing an ankle while I exercised to a walking aerobics DVD. It was easier for me to perform these calisthenics in the long foyer. I could see the TV and didn't have to navigate around furniture. Coop hid under a throw rug in front of the entry door and waited for me to execute a sidestep. When my leg was close enough, he lunged forward and grabbed an ankle. On one occasion I decided to use him as a weight. I lifted him above my head but could only manage two reps. It was like lifting a bag of rocks. My boy was solid muscle and bone. He must have thought the elevator ride was pretty cool because he didn't complain until I deposited him back on the floor. He stared up at me, anticipation beaming from his face. *When's the next ride?*

Cooper's Rule:
If you do something that gives
your mom the jitters, convince her
it's caffeine overload.

Chapter 21 COOPER'S 12-STEP PROGRAM FOR COMPULSIVE BEHAVIOR

I'm convinced November's chill ignited Cooper's winter anxiety. And, when he was anxious, I became a "victim by association."

It occurred to me Coop might benefit from the help of an animal behaviorist when red cat hair appeared on my living and dining room windows. Curious as I was about his "method of application," he'd reveal himself in due time and it wouldn't be a fond experience. Three years of co-habitation with Cooper had taught me as much.

It was nearly 3:00 a.m. when I was wrenched from my bed by the cracking sound of a dining room window. It barely contained the weight of a full-body thrust from a cat in need of Prozac. It was part of Cooper's modus operandi to introduce a particularly bizarre behavior in the wee hours of the morning. That's when I was most vulnerable to disturbances resembling a home invasion.

The flapping sound of my bare feet on the dining room floor didn't rustle a hair on his coat; the concentration on his subject was complete. He observed whatever his imagination conjured. Then he pounded his body against the window, obviously convinced it was the fastest way out. Finally, frustration got the better of him, and an angry *R-R-OWL* issued from deep in his throat and crescendoed off the walls.

"That's it." Feathery strands of red hair clung to the window like the wiry legs of a centipede. I swept Cooper into my arms, grateful he wasn't hemorrhaging from splintered glass. "Obviously, you're brain-damaged."

I realize my night vision can't compare to that of a cat, but there was nothing outside that could possibly have initiated this conduct. I wondered if my vet knew of any 12-step programs for compulsive behavior that applied to cats. I danced with threads of other possibilities contributing to this bad boy's habits. They proved too disturbing to assemble into thoughts.

Life with Cooper increased my chances of premature death. I knew this, but he was an addiction without means of control. I couldn't allow him to bash my windows any longer or eventually, he *would* break through. To my sleep-deprived brain, the path of least resistance was to plant him in the basement until morning when he could expend some energy in the great outdoors. WRONG ANSWER. Thirty minutes of body-slams against the basement door rattled the house and my nerves to the point of surrender.

I stormed through the kitchen and whisked the basement door open. "Why are you so naughty?" I asked the cat staring wide-eyed at me.

The adjective you're looking for is "spirited." Cooper's agile brain was a repository for excuses to match any behavior.

I brought him into bed and scratched his back. Just before we fell into an exhausted slumber, Cooper heard me whisper, "I see an exorcism in your immediate future."

Before dawn pierced the surface of my consciousness, I was

embroiled in a nightmare that involved my body and quicksand. I woke gasping for breath to find Coop sitting on my chest. The proud gleam in his eyes said *You're alive because I resuscitated you in time. You're welcome.*

"Cooper, you must be the reincarnation of someone I really pissed off in a former life."

***

Cooper's 12-Step Program For Compulsive Behavior

Step 1   Mom doesn't like live mice. I will only bring her dead ones.

Step 2   I will lick my hair off the windows.

Step 3   When Mom is in bed, she's sleeping, not unconscious. I won't sit on her chest to resuscitate her.

Step 4   I will let Chloe taste her food before I finish it.

Step 5   I will encourage Mom to cancel the exorcism by proving evil spirits don't control me.

Step 6   I will aim my fur balls at the floor, instead of Mom's pillow.

Step 7   I will hide Mom's toys where she can find them.

Step 8   I will stop blaming Chloe for my misdeeds.

Step 9   I will vacate Mom's sink the first time she asks.

Step 10   I will bury my deceased playmates.

Step 11   Each day, I will do one thing to make Mom happy she adopted me.

Step 12   I will ignore the previous 11 steps.

Cooper's Rule:
Deny everything.

Chapter 22   DR. JEKYLL AND MR. COOPER

In a rare calm moment, I found myself gazing deeply into the gold/green eyes of the man of my heart. He only allowed such close scrutiny because he was a hedonist, and I was administering a full-body massage.

Coop switched his rumbling purr machine to auto pilot and folded his eyes in slumber. "Stay with me," I pleaded. "I need those eyes to see into your soul. Why can't you be this sweetly content most of the time?" My queries carried him to dreamland.

Slumber that night was blessedly uneventful until I was awakened by the annoying prodding of a paw against my nose. Bloodshot eyes rolled to the clock radio.

"It's 3:30 in the morning, Cooper. The house better be on fire!"

I felt a hunger pang, was the message on his pinched face.

"Your food bowl is never empty."

I have a hankering for tuna. The pathetic expression he presented was meant to soften my heart and weaken my resolve.

This time it didn't work. " I have a hankering for filet mignon. Guess we'll both be disappointed."

What kind of mother are you? he had the temerity to ask.

"The normal kind who survives on sleep."

Animal Planet's cat whisperer, Jackson Galaxy, solves the problems of dueling cats. I wondered if his magic extended to those with strange neuroses.

Cooper's behavior followed a pattern based on the four seasons. He was reasonably sane during spring, summer and fall because he could prowl to his heart's content. His extreme insubordination surfaced when he was held captive inside during peak roaming hours.

Winter was the season of our discontent. As if below zero temperatures outside and forced-air heat inside weren't aging me fast enough, Cooper continued the usual winter rampages and found at least one new freakish behavior to add each year by the time the first snow fell. My shower liner was dotted with holes from his canines, and I was developing a nervous tick. I knew of doggie day care and needed to find the cat equivalent. Cooper would be the perfect candidate because he was a lover, not a fighter. The neighborhood ladies gravitated toward him, and he made buddies of the boys. Unfortunately for me, no such service exists.

The joke was on me when I set out to find an adult cat to adopt. And, of course, Chloe's sweet nature lulled me into a false sense of contentment. I raised my four Seattle cats from kittens. Having entered my sixties, I didn't have the patience or fortitude to survive the growing pains of another bambino. Yes, there's nothing cuter than kittens at play. But when they're jumping on your face at two o'clock in the morning, cuteness has a tendency to fade. Cooper was more work and caused more anguish than ten of the little critters. *Mom, you're too persnickety*, was a phrase I heard too often.

***

I scratched another winter off the calendar in blood and concentrated on a new challenge…the pit bulls next door. In a moment of madness, my neighbor allowed her irresponsible boyfriend to add two pit bull puppies to the menagerie they already had, a dog and two cats. The early scenario that played out in my imagination came to fruition when the dogs grew large and intimidating. Each time I needed to get into my garage, I phoned my neighbor and asked her to put King Kong (my name for him) inside. He was never tethered while outside, and I saw him as a lawsuit in waiting.

Kong's territory seemed to extend onto my property. He assumed a fighter's stance on top of the railing on her deck and growled and barked at me whenever I was in the back yard. One look at his rippling muscles, and the Green Bay Packers would have scouted him for their fall lineup.

I only allowed Cooper and Chloe outside when the coast was clear and kept an eye out for King Kong. One afternoon when I checked the deck for my cats, both Cooper and Chloe were plastered against the slider waiting for me to rescue them. Kong's bulging eyes scanned them from across the driveway. I quickly opened the door. As Cooper passed, I heard *That guy should be guarding San Quentin.*

One afternoon I glanced out the slider to find the pit bulls (brother and sister) snarling at each other in my back yard. Fear iced my body as I ran through the house to locate my cats. Chloe was inside, and Cooper was somewhere in the neighborhood. If he spied the dogs, I knew he wouldn't venture into the yard. I opened the slider and screen a crack so Coop could slip inside, if necessary, and was about to call my neighbor for help. By the time I picked up the phone, both dogs were inside my house. Obviously, they'd nosed the doors open far enough to slip into my home office.

We looked shocked to see each other in such close proximity. Thank the good Lord for home builders in the 1930's who added doors to every room. I quickly slammed the one between the hallway and kitchen closed so the dogs couldn't reach Chloe and me.

By the time my galloping fingers were calm enough to punch in my neighbor's phone number, the pit bulls had taken off. Earlier that day I witnessed a woman pushing a baby carriage past my neighbor's house while King Kong was loose in the back yard.

That afternoon drew me to the edge of my patience. Good neighborly relations were strained to the limit, and I seriously considered calling the police. I knew the dogs weren't licensed because we're only allowed to have two dogs and three cats in town.

This story might have had a happier ending if the pit bulls had been trained and properly restrained. Both of these young, healthy dogs were put down at the Humane Society when their owner lost interest in them.

> Cooper's Rule:
> If your mom catches you
> sipping the sauce, convince
> her it's for medicinal
> purposes.

Chapter 23   PARTY HARDY

My house sits in the ideal location for its inhabitants - across the street from a park and its related activities, and minutes from downtown, Rib Mountain shopping, and all the major highways. Historic neighborhoods, flush with ancient shade trees and burrows for wildlife, are most attractive to the four-legged residents. From time-to-time, when the 4th of July holiday rolls around, I invite friends to join me for a pizza party on my deck. It affords the best vantage point for the Marathon Park fireworks display.

On the most memorable occasion, Cooper enthusiastically agreed to host the festivities. Oddly enough, neither the strident explosions from illegal M-80's, nor the joyful bursts of psychedelic fireworks, frightened my cats. Chloe was allowed to participate from inside the protective screen door, while Cooper helped me entertain my guests on the deck. My first mistake was in not watching Coop like a hawk when careless friends slid a wine glass or beer bottle to the floor of the deck while they ooh-ed and ah-ed the magnificent display.

At some point in the evening, my friend, Ben, noticed Cooper lapping spirits from an unattended wine glass. I didn't realize until too late that my boy took his hosting duties seriously. In his mind, he would naturally partake of the libations. His raspy little tongue was too stubby to stretch down the long neck of a Corona bottle, but it didn't stop him from trying. I was alarmed when Coop staggered down the stairs, crouched in the grass, and projectile-vomited Merlo and Chardonnay across a wide expanse of lawn.

"Is he poisoned?" I asked my stunned guests, as fireworks blasted and Cooper barfed. Apparently, he'd managed a few bites of pizza that someone haphazardly left where he could devour it. Chunks of sausage added to the picturesque tableau peppering my grass. Glossy scraps of food resembled a Picasso abstract.

"It's coming up," Ben said. "He won't feel good, but he'll live."

I wasn't so sure. "I'm taking him to the emergency hospital."

My friend, Angie, chimed in. "You might want to wait 'til he's finished throwing up." Her husband, Ray, couldn't stop laughing.

I wanted to punch him for finding humor in Cooper's agony. I preferred the compassion shown by his brother, Ben, who didn't crack a smile.

"Let's wait and see how he is once it's all out. I'll bet he never sneaks booze again," Ben added.

"I won't take that bet." I glanced at Cooper, and our eyes locked briefly.

You could have warned me about the evils of alcohol and carbs, his shrunken face accused.

The fireworks display boasted its grand finale, but our party was over. The jovial spirit was marred by the tortured sounds of Cooper retching at least seven of his nine lives away. Poor Coop finished with a couple of dry heaves before exhaustion knocked him on his back. He needed a stint in rehab.

My guests were kind enough to clean up while I carried the little man to bed and watched over him through the night. I was nearly convinced a trip to the emergency room was imminent. I lay down beside Cooper but didn't touch him. He probably felt like every hair on his body was on fire.

"I'm sorry, buddy. It's my fault you're so sick. My friends aren't cat-proofed." His only response was a long, pathetic groan. I took it to mean *I'm done hosting your deadly parties.*

The photo that opened this chapter shows a pained face, still registering the effects of his hangover the next morning. He napped for a few hours, then bounced back to the boy I knew and loved. Soon after, he was outside terrorizing wildlife once again.

Cooper's Rule:
If your mom accuses you of
theft, convince her she's reading
too much John Grisham.

Chapter 24   THE NEIGHBORHOOD KLEPTOMANIAC

Cooper was an expert at convincing me I was losing my mind –
at least temporarily. I was in my home office pawing a glove that
didn't look familiar. That doesn't necessarily mean it wasn't mine, I
just couldn't quite place it. Let's pivot to the previous week, when a
pair of men's boxer shorts mysteriously appeared on the deck. There
was no doubt those babies weren't mine. I accused Coop of pilfering
from my neighbors' clothes lines. Instead of feeling shamed, his
whole body puffed with indignation. I felt like the reprobate who'd
just accused the Pope of stealing the Piscatory ring. When my deck
and back yard began to look like a consignment shop, I decided a
heart-to-heart was in order with my capricious boy.

"What's the deal, Coop? Can I expect a visit from the law on the
lookout for missing clothing and household items?"

His angelic face gazed at me from my bed, and I heard *I don't
understand you, Mom. I brought you a perfectly plump Mourning
Dove, my finest trophy. You tossed it back into the tree. And you
kept doing that until it magically disappeared. And what about
the mouse…a perfect toy for both of us? You hurled us out on the
grass. Now I bring you new clothes and you won't wear them.*

Not to mention the comb you flung into the trash. Humans are so confusing.

"Coop, I can't have neighbors knocking on my door looking for their belongings. It's only a matter of time until someone catches you making a getaway with their loot. The jig's up, buster. Your thieving days are over. You wouldn't want your mom to get stuck with community service because of your transgressions, would you?"

The fact he didn't answer, told me he'd get a chuckle out of watching me spear trash along the highway.

In no time, Cooper curbed his neighborhood scavenger hunts and re-applied his unique talents to picking pockets...or, in his case, ladies' purses. His test subject was my friend, Nancy. She and I were rehashing the "dumped boyfriend's addictions" when Nancy excused herself to use the facilities. She took her purse to freshen up and left it in the bathroom. This was a mistake since Cooper was inside catnapping. When anyone else was in the house, Coop kept one eye and ear alert for "opportunities."

While Nan and I chatted, Cooper ransacked her purse. He emptied the contents onto the floor and sorted through everything, no doubt nabbing gifts for me and toys for himself. When Nan went to retrieve her purse and found her belongings scattered everywhere, I felt obliged to crouch on the bathroom floor with her and feel around for contraband. We scrambled to recover a lipstick that rolled behind the toilet.

Nan was pallid, and therefore, compulsive about her makeup. She blended two lipstick colors and when we couldn't find her favorite, a Revlon Plumb, I offered to replace it. How I wished Cooper had an allowance I could confiscate to cover the cost. There was nothing the *Artful Dodger* could do to remedy my embarrassment but after Nan fled my house, I thought of a way to exact a little revenge.

"You're in timeout, Coop. I'm keeping you inside for the rest of the day, unless you can find Nan's lipstick in the next few minutes. Makeup isn't a hot commodity on the black market. Are you determined to abolish my social life by alienating all my friends?"

Let's negotiate I heard, before Coop jetted to the slider and yowled in protest.

"Use your *inside* voice, Cooper. I know you have one; I've heard it." I was determined to withstand whatever misery he planned for me to bat my point home.

***

Like many people I frown on solicitors who turn up at my door. Pick the most inconvenient time, and the doorbell will ring. On these occasions, I usually choose one of two courses of action: I ignore them, or open the door and growl. Both methods work well to discourage a second visit. As many of you know, nothing deters the mission of the Jehovah's Witness canvasser. With the exception of another great flood, they will always return. Such was my experience with Beatrice…until she encountered Cooper.

This lady rang my doorbell for a year. I finally folded and allowed her access. Even I can appreciate persistence born of piety. Although I no longer participate in organized religion, I pride myself in being a Christian who believes in God and respects and observes the tenets preserved in the Bible. Reared a Catholic, I didn't seriously consider changing my religion. Still, I saw nothing wrong in accepting the literature Beatrice offered and knew my dear, departed mother would be proud of the Bible study I was participating in.

While Beatrice and I spoke of the Lord, Cooper pawed at *The*

Watchtower pamphlets carelessly placed within reach. He soon began to devour a couple in a corner of the living room. The few he didn't ingest, he managed to leave crumpled and slobbered upon.

Beatrice and I were alerted to Cooper's sacrilegious behavior when he regurgitated a few wet pieces of *The Watchtower* onto my hardwood floor. As far as we could determine, nothing was stolen from either of Beatrice's bags, but Cooper had rifled through her things with no regard for propriety.

I was appalled by my cat's performance. It was clear Beatrice's own home was devoid of pets by her reaction to mine. She couldn't get out of my house fast enough. Evidently, worthier souls awaited salvation.

Cooper's Rule:
If you sneak a dog from another
house, convince your mom he
followed you home.

Chapter 25 **THE DOGNAPPER**

I glanced out the slider, as I did dozens of times a day, to see if Cooper wanted to come inside. The scene playing out in my back yard nearly stopped my heart. At first I registered a monstrous black wolf snacking on my cat. Once my brain caught up to my eyes, the wolf morphed into an intimidating Black Lab, and the attack, into a playful romp. It was one of the funniest encounters I've ever witnessed. Cooper sprinted up the French lilac tree and sprang onto the Lab's back. He miscalculated his target, because he fell off and rolled under his playmate.

When the Lab snorted and bounced from side-to-side, Cooper mimicked the maneuver, then raced in a circle around the back yard, followed closely by his new buddy. When one caught up to the other, they switched roles.

I knew the dogs on our block, and this guy didn't belong to any of my neighbors. Luckily, his tags were visible. I hoped he'd allow me to get close enough to read them and alert his owners.

Since Cooper's previous dognapping attempts had been thwarted, I assumed he'd moved farther on, where his reputation wouldn't precede him.

I watched the pair play until they tired and lay panting beside each other. Cooper rolled to his back and used all fours to scratch his companion under the chin. I drew a bowl of water and took it outside, deciding to survey the situation from the safety of my deck. The Lab's acceptance of my cat didn't necessarily transfer to a strange person.

"Hey, big guy. What's your name?" I asked the handsome fella. He stood and dropped his mouth open in a smile. When his tail spun like a propeller, I figured he wouldn't maul me if I moved closer. I put the bowl of water down beside the pals and offered my hand to the dog for a sniff. His long pink tongue slathered my hand with saliva, and he happily accepted a scratch behind his ears. I could see the name, Tucker, on his tag. While the two buddies slurped water, I returned to my home office and retrieved a pen and paper. The Lab was fine while I checked his tags and made note of his owner's name and phone number.

Cooper was in heaven. To him, we now had a dog.

Can we keep him? I heard.

"Not a chance," I replied. "You count as five pets. And besides, you have Chloe."

But I can't ride on her back.

"We aren't getting a dog just so you can ride on its back."

If the Lab's owners were anything like me, they'd be hyperventilating as soon as they noticed their dog was missing. I hustled back inside to give them a call.

"Is this Mrs. Miles?" I asked when a woman answered.

"Yes."

"Do you own a black Lab named Tucker?"

"Oh God, do you have him?"

"My cat brought him home. They've been playing in the back yard."

"My husband is driving around looking for him."

I gave the lady my address so she could call her husband and direct him to the right house.

Mr. Miles introduced himself as Jeremy, and he resembled a tall blade of grass. He was mighty happy to see Tucker in one piece. Man and dog were all over each other.

Cooper was the sad sack sitting behind me, contemplating the loss of his newest playmate.

"That's your cat?" Jeremy asked.

"Guilty," I replied.

"I chased him off my fence last week when I caught him lifting the latch."

"I'm so sorry." (I had apologized more since I adopted Cooper than at any other time in my life). "I was afraid he might have kidnapped your Lab. He's tried a few times with the neighbors' dogs. The Humane Society thought he'd shared one of his lives with a dog. I think he misses having a companion he can use for transportation."

Jeremy chortled. "Tucker plays with our cat, Lucy, but we keep her inside."

"I tried that with Cooper. It didn't fly. He'll spring Tucker again the first chance he gets."

"I'll put a lock on our fence. If your cat wants to play with Tucker in our yard, I don't have a problem with that."

"I'll try and convince him to observe your house rules." I swear there was a tear glistening in Cooper's eyes when Jeremy led Tucker to his car.

I had a brainstorm. I worried Jeremy would consider it more of a brain fart if I articulated my idea. But sometimes you just have to step out of the box. I was curious to learn how my cat had accessed the latch on their fence. "Would you mind if I brought Cooper over now to play with Tucker for a few minutes?"

Jeremy's face was blank, but no doubt his brain was hard at work calculating his wife's reaction to the dognapper returning to the scene of his crime.

"I'd like your wife to see Cooper in a more positive light and Frankly, I'm curious as to how the little scamp accomplished the deed."

"O-Okay. Let me give Linda a heads-up that we're on our way." He reached for the cell phone tucked in his back pocket.

"I have to get Cooper's carrier. He'll insist on driving if he's loose in the car." I allowed Jeremy to chew on that while I scampered back to the house. I wouldn't have been surprised to see taillights flash, as his car screamed away.

Jeremy was a true gent. He allowed the felon and me to follow him home. We meandered to Fifth Avenue via Callon Street. Linda was standing in the driveway of their bungalow when we arrived. She was the perfect bookend to her husband; nearly as tall and just as willowy.

I turned to Cooper. "You're lucky she isn't greeting us with a shotgun."

To the left of the driveway was a *For Sale by Owner* sign. After introductions were made and I apologized to Linda for my cat's thievery, Jeremy led us to their back yard. As soon as he opened the gate, Tucker raced inside. I opened the carrier so Cooper could follow. On his own, my little man had entered their back yard the same way he exited mine, by scooting under the fence. As to how he reached the latch, I spied his access point in the corner of their yard. A large woodpile sat against the fence with a blue plastic tarp covering it.

"There's the problem," I said. "Cooper climbed the woodpile to get to the latch." Jeremy and Linda both chuckled, and I smiled at my cat's cleverness. Why Tucker never used the woodpile to escape was beyond me.

"Where are you moving?" I asked, feeling sorry for my cat.

"Sussex," Jeremy said. "We have a lot of family in England and always planned to retire there."

On the way home, I broke the news to Cooper. "Those people are putting an ocean between you and their dog." I offered a silent prayer that my cat's dognapping days were over.

Cooper's Rule:
If you design a cat-inspired
clothing line, mimic the masters.

Chapter 26   COUTURE BY COOPER

For reasons only my crazy boy could understand, Cooper decided to design a cat-inspired clothing line. That's what I get for allowing him to watch the reality TV show, *Project Runway*. In his confused little mind, if aspiring fashion designers could compete each week, surely enterprising television executives could come up with a concept for cat contestants.

I discovered the result of his first fashion attempt on the floor of my hall closet. Evidently, I wasn't diligent enough in protecting my outerwear to close the door completely. Cooper seemed to find inspiration in my tan fall jacket and added a russet fur collar. He did a masterful job of combining knots of fur with silky strands to achieve his preferred rugged look. But without the help of a fashion consultant, he didn't realize saliva isn't an effective adhesive. When I picked up my jacket, Cooper's artistry drifted to the floor. He moved on to lingerie.

Although the drawers of my mirrored vanity aren't easy to open, a little muscle and a lot of determination can do the trick. Cooper was blessed with both. While I was unaware of a trickster at work, a couturier in the making practiced his happy dance on my unmentionables. He weaved designs deep into all the little nooks and crannies silky cat fur can inhabit.

When I caught him in the act, we had a conversation.

"Cooper, I can't think of a woman in the world who wants to wear hairy undies."

He leapt out of the drawer and tried to appear nonchalant. *Look at the unique patterns you have to choose from.*

One might think a cat with a propensity for fashion design would scrap an unsuccessful pursuit. You'd have to know mine to understand he'd make at least three futile attempts before he was out of the game.

Cooper was in the house and all was silent. This was cause for concern. I began my search with a loop of the main floor. A trail of toilet paper followed a route that had undoubtedly started in the bathroom. It wound through the kitchen and dining room, then back to whence it began. The culprit sat under the empty container wrapped like a mummy in Angel Soft toilet paper. Spit balls surrounded him on the floor. Cooper froze when he saw me, as if posing in situ made him invisible.

"There's quite a mess in here. Who would you conclude is responsible?" I asked, arms akimbo.

Chloe was the message on Coop's face.

"I don't think so, buster. Chloe's sleeping on the kitty condo. You, on the other hand, are wearing half a roll of toilet paper, and more evidence is dangling from your chin."

Are you gonna believe me, or your lyin' eyes? the little man offered.

"My lyin' eyes."

Cooper freed a paw from the ghostly roll of Angel Soft he wore like a Roman toga and brushed what was left of a spit ball from his chin.

"So. You had a few minutes on your hands and found a sudden urge to create a feline clothing line out of toilet paper?"

I prefer hardier material, but an artist uses the tools at his disposal was Cooper's excuse.

Cooper's Rule:
If your mom is too controlling,
fake a ghost sighting.

Chapter 27 THE GHOST AND THE SCARY MOVIE

Cooper wasn't above scaring the pants off his mom. Cats easily gauge the stress level in their humans, and my anxiety always shot to new heights while I was absorbed in a favorite pastime…horror movies.

My friends can't understand why I watch scary movies alone. Of course they frighten me, but I was battle-scarred early by my mother, an Alfred Hitchcock enthusiast. She took me to the drive-in to see *Psycho* when I was 12-years-old because none of her friends had the intestinal fortitude to watch Janet Leigh being filleted in the shower.

It was an unfortunate coincidence that on the night I watched *The Grudge,* a thunderstorm rumbled through Wausau, accompanied by torrential rain. Everyone knows the loudest claps of thunder occur during a particularly harrowing moment in any horror film. Cooper occupied my lap at the time. I can't tell you why the presence of a cat makes me feel immune to attack, but generally it does.

Maybe it was the fact I insisted Cooper stay inside that gave flight to his imagination. I'm sure he decided to have a little fun with me while I was so vulnerable to fear. He was familiar with the edgy soundtracks that accompany horror movies, as well as sighs that turn to high-pitched screams from characters about to be sliced into meat patties. I hugged the little warrior to my chest, and my heart hammered against his back. The visual of a dead Asian woman with a bad case of bed head, elbowing her way down a staircase toward Sarah Michelle Gellar, was singularly terrifying. Suddenly, Cooper's head whipped to the right; mine whipped in unison to confront whatever unimaginable apparition loomed behind my chair. Cooper's gaze froze above my head. I was one incident away from blacking out.

"What is it, Coop? What do you see?" I begged frantically.

He stared, his pupils dilating. *You don't want to know*, I heard.

My head lashed in every direction, freeing my hair to beat the heck out of my face. I was prepared to toss Cooper at whatever lurked nearby, convinced my cat's ninja skills would save us both.

When I began to pant, Cooper may have thought he'd taken his joke a little too far. The combination of a storm, a horror movie, and a ghost could render him an orphan. He eased up on the rotating stare and relaxed into my lap; a sign that present danger had flickered out like a breathless candle. The only thing left to fear was the ghostly woman trapped inside the TV screen.

Cooper taught his unique skills to Chloe. At least one of them used the "ghost stare" to unnerve me when they felt the need to teach me a lesson. Sometimes they worked together, staring for long moments into a corner of the room or at a point high on the wall, to indicate the ghost about to annihilate me was nearly nine feet tall. The gold medal went to the cat who focused attention on the space behind me, unsettling me enough to spin in a circle to confront an assailant my cats had drawn from my vivid imagination. All of this only etched another wrinkle into my feline-worn face; one of the many hazards of sharing a home with a wily cat and his willing accomplice.

> Cooper's Rule:
> If a new cat wants to join
> your posse, make him walk in
> your shadow.

Chapter 28   **ONE BAD APPLE**

The witching hour was upon us, but there was no sign of my incorrigible boy. He wasn't on the deck, so I traipsed through the house to the front door. When I opened it, a new scenario was playing out. Cooper had found an adversary. A bloated gray cat with a bad attitude sat on my neighbor's retaining wall and hissed profanities at my boy. Cooper pulled a Rocky Balboa standoff in the driveway. These two guys spat testosterone with every hiss and yowl. It was time for me to referee.

"Come on in, Coop."

He glanced at me, and I heard *But Mom, he's calling me names.* He turned his attention back to Bruiser (my name for the combatant) and arched his back, while walking sideways toward his opponent.

"Get in here, Cooper."

Now he's swearing at me, Cooper complained. He kept his back to me, but edged toward home.

My cat didn't have enemies. If he could bewitch raccoons,

strange dogs, and all the ferals who'd found our house over the years, what was different about this new guy, I wondered. He must be an alien cat from a planet immune to Cooper's charm. For the moment, Bruiser seemed more interested in my reaction to their power play than to Cooper, who was at least one size smaller.

"Ding-Ding. That's the bell ending round three, Coop. It's time to come inside."

Obviously trying to save face, Cooper stood his ground. *He has to leave first,* I heard him mutter.

Bruiser glanced from me to Cooper, and seemed bored. These dudes weren't going to rumble with a mom watching.

The porch light was on. Some of the moths dancing in the soft glow decided my open door was an invitation to flit inside. As dusty wings fluttered past my face, the last of my patience evaporated. I stomped down two steps, and the boys scattered in opposite directions. My actions gave Cooper the excuse he needed to bolt for the door. Bruiser had launched first and that's all that mattered.

"We're gonna have a talk," I said to Cooper's tail, as he rounded the corner to his food bowl. Chloe stumbled into our disagreement and made a beeline for the home office. She wasn't about to be caught in the line of fire.

I guess Cooper thought the crunching sounds he exaggerated would ward off my anger. He looked surprised when I picked him up and hugged him tight. I breathed in the smoky scent of his fur. He'd been at someone's cookout. My only concern was that he and Bruiser had tussled before I spotted them. I carried Coop to my bed and inspected his fur and limbs for any signs of bites, blood or missing hair. He passed my keen inspection, and I let him resume his meal.

I'll bet it wasn't two days later when I caught sight of Cooper bouncing down the sidewalk. Bruiser followed close behind. I swear they hummed *Kumbaya* in lock step. Guess they'd buried the hatchet, but I couldn't imagine how my cat had convinced Bruiser that he was merely a serf in Cooper's kingdom.

Cooper's Rule:
Sometimes you just have
to relax and watch the
clouds roll by.

Chapter 29 COOPER'S MISCHIEVOUS MAMA

I was either feeling playful or channeling Cooper. A fiendish desire to join the conversation two women were having about their toddlers got the best of me. Besides, what else is there to do in the waiting room of a dentist's office?

"We're at our wits end trying to potty-train Evan," said Mother Number One, a mousey blonde.

"Boys take longer; be patient. You don't want to scar him for life," said Mother Number Two, a nerdy-looking brunette. In the brief silence that followed, she adjusted her eyeglasses as if she couldn't find a comfortable fit.

I took my cue from the lull in conversation. "My little Cooper was potty-trained in infancy," I interjected, gloating. Their heads snapped in my direction, and two sets of eyes drilled holes into my forehead.

Mother Number One, probably feeling more pressure since her son was the slacker, spoke first. "That's impossible!"

Mother Number Two quickly came to her defense. "I've never heard of such a thing either, especially with boys."

This was devilishly fun. "On the contrary, my Cooper mastered everything early. He's only six and already converses in different languages with friends of many species."

The two women exchanged a snotty glance.

The clue I tossed them with the word, *species*, didn't seem to land. "Just before I left to come here, I coaxed him off the roof of our garage. He was observing a Blue Jay." The light still didn't switch on. I smelled the pungent odor of smoke while they burned me at the stake.

Mother Number One, the most combative, sparred with me. "What kind of woman allows a six-year-old boy to sit on the roof? How did he even get up there?" Her eyebrows tented above startled eyes.

"He climbed the tree next to our garage," I said. "I'm a strong believer in freedom of expression."

Mother Number One's fingers twitched. I envisioned her snatching her cell phone and punching in the number for Child Protective Services.

A chuckle tickled my throat, and I caved. "Did I mention Cooper has four legs and a tail? He's my cat." There was definitely scorched earth around our chairs, and that was the bitter end of my conversation with the ladies. Still, I couldn't help feeling like the victim of misplaced aggression. Where was their sense of humor?

In the dental chair, my mouth stuffed with cardboard, I giggled like a lunatic. It's a wonder the technician was able to get decent x-rays. I worried I'd swallow the mouth pieces and choke to death before I could tell Cooper about the chaos Mama had caused at the dentist's office. Some of Cooper's antics had definitely rubbed off on his mother. So…I was only guilty by association.

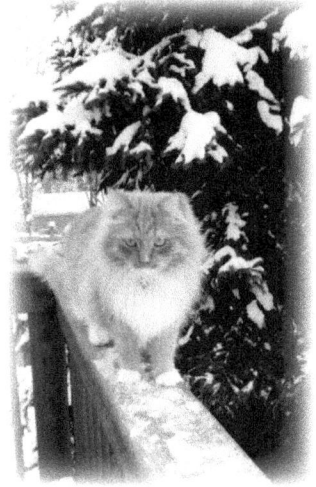

Cooper's Rule:
If your mom insists on a curfew, tell
her rules are made to be broken.

Chapter 30   COOPER'S COUP

Here comes the big reveal. I became convinced Cooper was making plans to kill me in my sleep. The giveaway was a furtive and vengeful glance tossed my way each evening, especially when we were hunkered down in bed for the night.

Knowing Cooper as I did, he'd cultivate a garden of ideas, but would have difficulty settling on the right method. I knew he'd wish to dispatch me with the least amount of discomfort…or maybe all he really cared about was a convincing alibi.

Chloe was his stooge. He tested a fake kill on her. The smothering backfired badly. Chloe was bigger; she simply shimmied out from under him and swatted him senseless. Cooper walked softly and carried a big stick after that. He didn't enjoy the pummeling and learned to slink in and out of rooms without notice. He was very good at subterfuge.

Surely, dispensing of his mother wasn't his first choice. He merely ran out of options to control me. I was too insistent on his observing my 7:00 p.m. curfew.

It was during this time that the conspirator stopped all conversation, as if he were afraid he'd reveal himself by appearing too "chatty." But, a mother always knows when one of her kids is up to no good. It was my duty to draw him out, uncover his schemes, and shame him enough to discourage further antics.

I tried hypnotism; it only irritated him. He swatted the shiny bauble away from his face and stormed out of the room. I saw my opportunity a couple of nights later while Coop was stretched out on my lap. He was a compliant captive during back scratches.

"Coop, we need to talk."

He rolled onto his back so I could attend to his chest and tummy. *Keep scratching*, he sighed.

"Is there murder in your heart?" I asked, a hitch in my voice.

His scrunched face begged the question, *Say what?*

"Are you plotting a coup d'etat against your mom? That's no way to get into Heaven, Coop."

He rolled onto his stomach, pushed himself into a sitting position, and froze. A light switched on when he realized this wasn't going to be a casual session. The little connectors in his cat brain fired brightly. I saw sparks in his eyes. *Wha-what do you mean?* I read in his confused expression.

"Did you try a practice smother on Chloe?"

He lowered his head. *She wouldn't stop gabbing. I only tried to muffle her.*

I felt tension in his body but continued anyway. "So…you're not trying to get rid of me?"

He shook his head. *Mom! How can you ask such a question? You may be a little slow on the uptake, but everyone knows you don't liquidate the hand that feeds you.*

"What about the tripping incident?"

You're clumsy. He had me on that one.

You keep trying to blur the line between Master and Staff. I had to figure out a safe way to neutralize you at night so I could stay out late without worrying you. Chloe was supposed to help, but she's not clever enough to grasp the concept of "diversionary tactics." The earnest look on his face convinced me.

No longer under threat of death, I lifted Cooper into my arms and hugged him tight. He even allowed a big smooch on his cheeks. My boy and I were back to loving each other unconditionally. The feeling was grand.

Cooper's Rule:
A raised paw is a cat's stop sign.

Chapter 31   **TELL IT TO THE PAW**

I began to contemplate a lobotomy for Cooper as the only way to gain dominion over him. His willfulness was legendary, but the last straw was when he raised a paw in my direction or touched it to my lips, and I heard *Talk to the paw.* It was his way of putting an end to my rant. Once again, I admonished him for coming in late. He offered a new excuse.

My Homies and I are the neighborhood watch. We patrol so you can sleep in peace.

"I can't sleep at all until you're in the house."

Two days later I trolled the neighborhood close to midnight, calling his name. Hot, angry veins protruded from my forehead as I spat "Cooper!" up and down empty streets. It was a Tuesday night, and many of my neighbors rose early for various jobs. That was the reason I dialed down the volume of my screeches.

Pacing back and forth along Stewart Avenue, like a hooker down on her luck, I took one last glance up 7th Avenue and spotted my prey. Cooper's eyes caught mine, and the showdown began. He knew enough about my body language to detect fury in my stance.

"Cooper!" I called. He made me feel like a woman dragging her husband home from his favorite pub.

The punk froze, and I knew he was scanning his options.

"Guess you heard me wailing like a banshee. Get over here, so we can go home."

When my hands met my hips, Cooper began to advance in my direction. He took slow, tentative steps toward me while I fumed. When he reached my side, I came unglued. My arms flailed in every direction, and I babbled incoherently. Cooper probably thought his mother was speaking in tongues and had finally gone over to the dark side.

He jetted toward the house, and I heard, *If my Home Boys see me with you in your present state, I'll lose all credibility.*

"You better not even detour long enough to sniff a bug, buddy boy!"

While I traipsed through the front door, Cooper scampered to the back. It was an act of self-preservation to put a house between us until I calmed down. After several gulps of air and the obligatory scratch under my good cat's chin, I was ready to face the devil peering at me through the glass slider. We gazed into each other's eyes for a moment with separate thoughts, then I opened the door. Cooper sauntered inside and wrapped his downy tail around my leg. I was a sucker for his special hugs. Like every scalawag, he knew how to smooth the bumps in his road.

Sometimes Cooper acted like keeping him inside at night was the equivalent of a zombie apocalypse. "What exactly are you trying to accomplish out there?" I asked.

World domination was his reply.

"Famous last words," I countered.

On the way to his food bowl I heard, *Sorry, Mom, but a guy's gotta do what a guy's gotta do.*

When we were finally tucked into bed, I opened my mouth to deliver the last word. Cooper felt my breath on his face, and beat me to the punch. He placed a velvet mitten against my lips. *Tell it to the paw*, I heard.

Chapter 32   **GONE**

It's embarrassing to admit I was outfoxed by my cat. Cooper set his own parameters. He usually came inside between 5:00 and 6:00 p.m. for a snack. I began keeping him inside at that time to avoid his midnight jaunts and my subsequent rants.

Fine, he no doubt thought. *I'll skip the snack and stay outside so Mom can't trap me in the house.* This became a game he wildly favored. He never missed an opportunity to put one over on his mom.

Spring was the worst because Cooper relished his freedom after months inside watching his territory recede under a blanket of snow.

Again, I paced in front of the glass slider at 3:00 a.m. searching for a cat who had no consideration for his mom's gray hair (adroitly camouflaged by Revlon's Colorsilk No. 45). I scurried to the front door and opened it. No sign of wildlife or a delinquent ginger cat. Back and forth in the wee hours of morn – that was my routine with Cooper.

Rounding the corner into my home office, I spied two pink and white paws pressed against the glass. I drew closer.

Coop gauged anger by the set of my features. He could tell he needed to schmooze big-time. The show began. He pressed his face against the glass. *Look at me*, his expression said, *Aren't I adorable? You know you can't stay mad at me when I'm so-o-o cu-u-t-e. Who's your boy? Who do you love?* And all the while, he danced from side-to-side, turned so he could toss a coy glance over his shoulder, and generally charmed the wrath out of my soul.

I opened the door and scooped him up. His motor rumbled against my chest, as I breathed in the cool night air on his fur.

"You're going to be the death of me, Coop." This was a message he heard so often it had obviously lost its impact. Still, I felt it necessary to pour on the guilt. "I hope you know your personal freedom is shortening my life." He wrapped fleecy arms around my neck and purred. We hugged each other tight. As a little bonus, Cooper was a good boy for the next two days, ending his travels by 9:00 p.m.

Two days as a good boy were all Coop could manage. The call of the wild was as seductive to him as the Siren's song to ancient mariners.

It was Thursday, June 5, 2014. Another night of pacing to no avail. Cooper didn't come home at all. This felt different somehow, like being on a roll in Vegas, then betting on red when the ball lands on black.

I wasn't familiar with all of Coop's haunts, but on Friday I traced the paths he typically followed on a daily basis; this included all the neighborhood streets and alleys. I attached his name to every breeze so he'd hear my voice wherever he might be. I found solace in the fact there were no signs of violence – no fur, no blood, no body. Still, my Cooper, my little boy, man of my heart, was gone without a trace.

By the second day, I was frantic. I snaked around garages calling his name. He could have gotten trapped inside at night. Why didn't he answer my call? I knocked on doors with his photo. I posted flyers everywhere that would take them – called all my friends and neighbors so they'd watch for him. I drove for miles in every direction calling his name out the windows. Where was he?

By day three I was sobbing uncontrollably. The worst scenarios tortured my mind. What if he was trapped somewhere and couldn't find his way out? Could he be in a moving van headed out of state or out of the country? He loved the view from rooftops. What if an eagle's talons caught hold of him?

"Cooper, please come home!" I cried.

I grasped hope with every fiber of my being, clinging to stories of cats who'd found their way back home from other states. Lying in bed at night, the whisper of leaves dusting the deck stairs spoofed the soft patter of Cooper's paws. That sound sent me flying to the door begging God to see his face through the glass. I made pilgrimages to the slider every few minutes desperately searching for any sign of my lost boy.

Like a detective, I tried to piece together the last moments anyone had seen Cooper so I could place him somewhere in those final hours and figure out what happened to him.

Animal control didn't have any casualties that fit Cooper's description. He hadn't been taken to the Humane Society or any animal hospital in the area. I plastered his picture online.

My neighbor, Ted, had been out of town for the weekend. I told him Cooper disappeared Thursday night. He mentioned seeing him in the parking lot across the street at about 8:30 that night. He called to him, and said Coop dropped on his back and performed his happy dance. Then he bounded across the street and headed toward my back yard. That was the last time anyone saw him.

I was guilt-ridden hearing this. Did Cooper come to the slider when I wasn't there to let him in? Patience wasn't his strong suit; in moments he would have taken off again. The night held irresistible attractions.

Within the first week, leads began to roll in. A man saw his picture at County Market and called to say there was an orange and white cat for adoption at PetsMart. The timing didn't seem right, but I sped to PetsMart anyway. I followed any trail that might lead to Cooper, my heart filled with expectation. The cat I saw barely held any resemblance to mine. He was a short-haired kitten, mostly white with patches of ginger. People mean well, but I don't think they focus on details in a photo.

A lady who lived on 9th Avenue phoned to say a cat matching Cooper's description was coming to her house to eat. I assured her it wasn't my boy. If he was in the neighborhood, he'd come home. What if he had amnesia? I called the woman back and asked her to describe the cat in detail. It was larger than Cooper and a short-hair. The quest to find my little man continued.

Two weeks passed and still no sign of Cooper. I cried so wretchedly I made myself ill and was bedridden for two days. Why was there no sign of him anywhere? Then I tried to take comfort in that fact. Not having a body meant he was still out there. But where?

Mechanically, I dragged myself back and forth from one end of the house to the other. I searched for Cooper through every window and doorway. I couldn't eat. I couldn't sleep. My body was an empty vessel, all the life sucked out by grief. I begged God to bring my boy home. Not knowing what happened to him was worse than anything my imagination could conjure.

If there was any way for Cooper to get back to me, he would use every ounce of strength his little body could muster to come home. Cooper was the sunshine of my life.

I was adrift in a nightmare with no sign of reprieve.

Chapter 33   **HEARTBROKEN**

After three agonizing weeks with no sign of Cooper, my telephone rang. I was washing a coffee cup and listened to the message.

"My name is Cindy Schulz. I just saw your cat's picture at County Market…"

I dropped the half-washed cup and loped to the phone. My hands were wet. I dried them hastily on my jeans and hit the talk button on the wall phone.

"Yes, I'm here," I breathed.

"Oh. Hi." She paused, perhaps thinking I was about to say something else.

I could barely breathe trying to anticipate what this lady would say.

"I'm positive your cat's the one I took off Stewart Avenue. He'd been hit and killed."

My stomach dropped to the floor, and my mouth felt like the Sahara Desert. *No! It couldn't be my Cooper. I tested him. He never went near Stewart Avenue. Too much traffic, too much noise. Coop was a stray before I adopted him. He had street smarts.* My thoughts were jumbled together. Denial was easy.

"I don't think it was my cat. Other people called me with leads, but none of them turned out to be Cooper." My hands were clammy. I tucked the phone between my chin and shoulder and rubbed them hard against my jeans. I needed details, yet was terrified to ask. The lady seemed to sense as much in the silence at my end of the line.

"There was very little blood. I think he was clipped by a car and killed instantly. He was on his side and looked like he was asleep. I must have passed him shortly after it happened."

There was a fail-safe way to determine whether the cat she found was mine. "Can you tell me the color of his collar?" Cooper had lost another collar the day he disappeared. I put Chloe's iridescent pink one on him until I could get a new name tag. It was important he carry my contact information with him.

"It was pink and shiny."

Life drained from my body. I moved like a radio-controlled robot. "It was his collar."

"We found it about four feet away from him but couldn't find the tag. It haunted us. I can show you a picture of the collar. We posted it online."

She described his collar perfectly, but I still needed to see the picture.

"I'm at County Market now. If you want to meet me here, I'll show you exactly where we found him. Maybe we can find the tag in daylight."

She didn't need to convince me. I snatched my car keys off the hook and fled.

When I arrived at County Market, I probably looked like a somnambulist. My reactions were sluggish, and I didn't say much. Part of me was somewhere else. Although I heard everything she said to me, I couldn't be sure how much truly registered.

I followed Cindy to the scene of the accident. She explained that she was driving home from a church social when she spotted Cooper's body on the other side of the median.

Stewart Avenue is a four-lane thoroughfare divided in the middle by a grassy median. It separates Marathon Park from the homes on the other side.

By the time Cindy was able to turn around and get to Cooper, another car had pulled over, and four young CNA's were already standing next to him. One young girl sobbed. Cindy asked her if they had hit the cat. She said, "No. He's just so beautiful."

The group agreed to move Cooper off the road and onto grass near the sidewalk on 5th Avenue. Cindy found a plastic bag inside the trunk of her car. They placed Cooper on top of it and gently moved him onto the grass. Cindy called police. While waiting for an officer, five Good Samaritans rooted through their vehicles for flashlights and searched for Cooper's ID tag. Most of the participants had cats at home and were desperate to locate this one's owner.

My body was leaden, as though I were coming out of anesthesia. "Cooper disappeared three weeks ago; on Thursday, June 5th."

"That's when we found him. About 10:30 that night," Cindy said.

"So, he was already dead. I can't tell you what I've gone through the past three weeks not knowing what happened to him. I lay in bed at night straining for the sound of his little paws racing up the steps to my deck. I almost convinced myself he'd gotten trapped inside someone's moving van and was on a journey back home."

"I urged the officer to take him to the Humane Society so they could scan him for a microchip. We could see he was a well-cared-for cat and someone would look for him," Cindy said.

"I'll call the police when I get home and find out where they took Cooper. They should have a record of their stop that night." This wasn't the conclusion I'd prayed for. "I'll never be able to thank you enough for moving him off the road. If you hadn't, I would have found his body in the morning. By then, who knows how many cars would have rolled over him."

"We couldn't leave him there. We all hope someone would do the same for us. Even the police officer helped us look for the ID tag. We searched for twenty minutes."

Cindy and I made our own effort to find any sign of Cooper's ID tag, but without success. The tag was a thin piece of metal. It was probably pulverized in the accident.

The final confirmation that my little guy had met his end on Stewart Avenue was in the photo of his collar that Cindy showed me.

Tragic as the situation was, both of us were relieved it was finally resolved. While I was on my way to County Market to meet her, Cindy had sent an e-mail message to notify the young girl in the other car that she'd found the cat's owner.

Cindy returned home with me and took a snapshot of the picture of Cooper gracing page 45 of this book. She e-mailed it to the young girl who had cried so hard next to him the night they found him. The caption read, "This WAS her cat. His name was Cooper."

I'd offered a reward in my flyer. Cooper's angels wouldn't accept payment for their kindness.

My sorrow was sharpened after I returned home and phoned the police. The officer I spoke with looked up the incident report for the night of Cooper's death. I needed to know if there was any way I could still recover his body.

"It's my understanding you scan cats for microchips, whether or not they're alive. I adopted Cooper from the Humane Society. They microchip all cats and dogs when they're adopted."

"I'm sorry, Ma'am, we're just now beginning that training."

"What do you do with the bodies of animals who are hit by cars?" I asked.

"The officer on duty would have left him in the nearest dumpster."

Fresh tears lined my eyes. "So, he's in a landfill somewhere."

His silence was the answer.

This shattered my heart. Not only was Cooper gone, but I couldn't even offer him a proper burial.

Searching frantically for any tangible sign of him, I regretted being a clean freak. Finding a clump of Cooper's fur would have been a treasure. I was desperate for his scent. His fur always smelled like a spring day, fragrant with his travels.

I remembered the shower liner. Dashing into my bathroom, I pushed aside the nylon curtain and found signs of Cooper I needed to see. Puncture marks from his canines dot the surface of that liner. I followed their pattern with my fingertips, remembering each event. Tears fell as I traced his four winters, further evidence of Cooper's unique history.

Epilogue   ## LIFE WITHOUT COOPER

Gaze into the soulful eyes of your cat, and you'll see a reflection of love, a bounty of curiosity, a zeal for life, and a spark of impishness. I wanted to see Cooper again. And I do see him everywhere. When I glance out the front windows, he's sitting at the end of my driveway, as he did so often, deciding the direction in which his greatest adventure will materialize. I glimpse him on tiptoe on the settee searching through the dining room windows for a mouse or squirrel to harass. In another moment, his apparition is rounding the corner to his food bowl, or softly snoring in a sunbeam.

Cooper flavored my life. Sometimes he was Sweet Basil and oftentimes, Cayenne Pepper.

It's just us girls now; no scrappy boy to liven our nights and color our days. Even Chloe felt the loss, initially. She often stared out the slider wistfully, and I heard her wonder *Where's Cooper? Why doesn't he come home?* There was no one to take her on safari anymore, no mouse spinning before her eyes, no one to lie beside her on grass scented by a spring rain. The rainbows in her days with Cooper were missing.

Life is a series of hills and valleys. Mine was stranded in a deep valley. I couldn't get past Cooper's death. A friend asked if I regretted allowing him to roam. My response was one of profound certainty…absolutely not. If we could have seen the future, and Cooper understood his choices, a life of safety inside or four years of wonders outside, I can hear him clearly. *I'll take those four years and make the most of them.* And he did. His territory was wide. To experience his world through a pane of glass would have been agonizing for a cat like Cooper. Not to pound the earth with his presence as he thundered through the neighborhood, or smell the profusion of scents riding every breeze, or experience the subtle signs of one season melding into another, wasn't a life he would have chosen for himself.

I never worried about Stewart Avenue because it was so busy during the day. My problem was failing to recognize the opening Cooper would have seen. After about 9:00 p.m., traffic eases exponentially with each passing hour. Cooper was the cat equivalent of Lewis and Clark. He loved discovering new territory. The proliferation of squirrels in Marathon Park must have beckoned him. I have no doubt he felt invincible because everyone made concessions for him. He was the master of his kingdom.

Writing this book serves two purposes: it pays homage to a special cat and acts as a catharsis for his mom. I began writing in earnest on the one-year anniversary of Cooper's death. An earlier attempt fell by the wayside. The emotional turmoil was too great.

Life continues for Chloe and me, although much of its richness disappeared with Cooper. I'm still caring for feral cats, while Chloe delights in her role as princess. She now has a sister she'd just as soon drown.

For too-short a time we were blessed with a companion named Cooper. While straining our patience at times, he entertained us with his high jinks, taught us the meaning of a life well-lived, and never failed to demonstrate the depth of his love. If there were ever a cat that infused all nine lives with fervor, Cooper was his name.

My little man is greatly missed, but never forgotten. Pictures grace my home with his presence. Cooper shines from the refrigerator, from my writing desk, from this book, and always, from my heart.

ACKNOWLEDGEMENTS

I'm so grateful to my first reader, extraordinary author, Sandra Kring, for her exceptional eye, encouragement and friendship. She shares her time and talents most generously.

Thanks to Nancy, Irene, Shirley, Karyn and Mark, my Central Wisconsin Creative Writers critique group, for their unique skills at pulling the best out of any piece of art.

I'd be remiss if I didn't acknowledge Shannon and Lauren at Ten16 Press for giving life to my greatest labor of love.

ABOUT THE AUTHOR

Chari Fish is a member of Central Wisconsin Creative Writers and has volunteered as a literacy tutor for functionally illiterate adults. She lives in North Central Wisconsin with her two cats, Chloe and Nevaeh. *He Had Me at Meow* is her nonfiction debut. Visit Chari on Facebook, Instagram, and Twitter.